Training Shootir

Name: _____

Birthday: _____

Address: _____

_____

School/Grade: _____

_____

Photo

Club: _____

Discipline: _____

Motto: _____

_____

Training Shooting Sports

Katrin Barth & Beate Dreilich
Sports Science Consultant:
Dr. Berndt Barth

Meyer & Meyer Sport

Original title: Ich trainiere Sportschießen
© Meyer & Meyer Verlag, 2010

Translated by Petra Haynes
AAA Translation, St. Louis, Missouri, USA
www.AAATranslation.com

British Library Cataloguing in Publication Data
A catalogue record for this book is available from the British Library

Training Shooting Sports
Katrin Barth & Beate Dreilich
Maidenhead: Meyer & Meyer Sport (UK) Ltd., 2011
ISBN: 978-1-84126-305-2

All rights reserved. Except for use in a review, no part of this publication maybe reproduced, stored in a retrieval system, or transmitted, in any form or by any means now known or hereafter invented without the prior written permission of the publisher.
This book may not be lent, resold, hired out or otherwise disposed of by way of trade in any form, binding or cover other than that which is published, without the prior written consent of the publisher.

© 2011 by Meyer & Meyer Sport (UK) Ltd.
Auckland, Beirut, Budapest, Cairo, Cape Town, Dubai, Graz, Indianapolis, Maidenhead, Melbourne, Olten, Singapore, Tehran, Toronto
Member of the World
Sport Publishers' Association (WSPA)
www.w-s-p-a.org
Printed by: B.O.S.S Druck und Medien GmbH
ISBN: 978-1-84126-305-2
E-Mail: info@m-m-sports.com
www.m-m-sports.com

Content

1. **Dear Shooting Sport Athlete** 9
   Tips from the authors, sports and art

2. **Interesting Facts About Shooting Sports** 13
   Shooting sports disciplines, competitions, American and international organizations

3. **Hi There, Petra!** 19
   A conversation with Petra Horneber, the successful German shooting athlete, fan pages

4. **Training – the Road to Success** 23
   Training, training correctly, goals, motivation, physical workload, what it takes to be a successful shooting athlete, training diary

5. **Physical Fitness and Coordination** 39
   Physical fitness in general, physical fitness in shooting sports, endurance, strength, speed, flexibility, fitness training, reaction speed drills, flexibility exercises, coordination, coordination exercises

6. **It's All in the Mind** 57
   The brain – our computer, perception, reflexes, attitude, coping with nervousness, fear and anger, overcoming difficulty, alertness, concentration, pressure, relaxation, self-confidence, competitive strength, exercises, test

7. **Technique** 79
   General technique, technique in shooting sports, technique training, increased performance, training tips, monitoring, evaluation, muscle sense, sensitization program

Training Shooting Sports

| 8 | **Rifle Shooting** .... .89 |

Standing firing position, prone firing position, kneeling firing position, taking aim, firing, follow-through, breathing

| 9 | **Pistol Shooting** ....111 |

Precision shooting, motion sequence and technical elements, breathing, taking aim, firing, rapid-fire shooting

| 10 | **Safety First!** ....131 |

Rules, firearm safety, shooting sport regulations, making a case against firearm misuse and for the sport

| 11 | **Fit and Healthy** ....139 |

Performance capacity, eating and drinking right, energy sources, prevention and regeneration, doping

| 12 | **Solutions** ....147 |

Solutions and answers to brain teasers

| 13 | **Let's Talk!** ....149 |

Dear Parents, Dear Trainer, some suggestions from the authors regarding the use of this book

Photo & Illustration Credits 152

Please note:

The exercises and practical suggestions in this book have been carefully chosen and reviewed by the authors. However, the authors are not liable for accidents or damages of any kind incurred in connection with the content of this book.

For the purpose of better readability we have decided to use only the male (neutral) form of address throughout the book, which of course also includes the female gender.

Training Shooting Sports

"Hi there! I'm Sammy, the little stork with the long accurate beak! You may even remember me from the book "Learning Shooting Sports"."

"And now you're ready to properly train with a rifle or a pistol? Ok, I'll be at your side once again!"

"And of course I will be there, too!"

Training Shooting Sports

Helpful symbols in this book

The thumb means we have a great tip for you. Advice or mistakes are pointed out to you.

Here you will find brainteasers or questions.

The answers and solutions are at the back of the book.

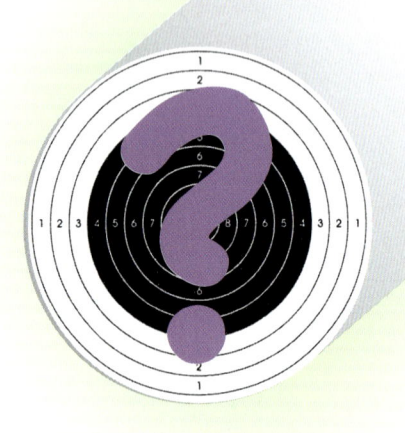

Here you will find something to record, fill in or check off.

. . . 1 Dear Shooting Sport Athlete

You started out with the fundamentals of shooting sports and now you have already learned the basics. Maybe you even practiced with our beginning book "Learning Shooting Sports". Now you regularly train at a club, have learned a lot, and have competed in your first competitions. If you are now interested in this training book and are reading it, we can assume that you are still very enthusiastic about this great sport. You want to continue on and train properly and with purpose.

You want to be more focused, have more endurance and be more accurate. Familiar techniques are built upon and new ones are added. You want to gain personal experience and make individual adjustments to the techniques.

Although not everyone around you always appreciates your sport of choice, you recognize the personal athletic challenge. You don't have to be overly strong, tall, thin or attractive. Your performance can be physically measured and you are therefore not dependent on the sympathy of referees. It is an indoor and outdoor sport; you do not have to hurt anyone and don't have to push yourself to your absolute physical limit. Valuable qualities such as the ability to concentrate, determination, sagacity and resolve are cultivated. The special sports equipment causes you to be very responsible and cautious.

Training Shooting Sports

But first a little story:

A strapping boy was visiting the mountains and wanted to climb a high peak. Cheerfully he packed food and drink, and started to hike with a bounce in his step.

Since he wasn't familiar with the route he made slow progress. He climbed up and when he realized that he couldn't get any further, he had to turn back and start over. These detours cost him lots of strength. Sometimes he got lucky and found a trail that brought him a little closer to the top. After many such attempts he finally reached the summit, only to realize that others were already there. They told him about a good hiking trail. He could have taken that without all those detours.

Why didn't he use a map or ask someone who had already taken this hike?

Training in shooting sports is similar to our story about the "conqueror of the peaks". Many shooting athletes have trained before you and some have become very successful. So you don't have to reinvent shooting sports and shooting training, but rather learn from the experiences of shooting athletes before you. That will make it much easier for you.

The training book "Training Shooting Sports" will provide you with a kind of "trail map" and a little tutorial on how you can climb the "shooting athlete's peak" without making a lot of detours. And of course there's your trainer who can show you the right way.

It sometimes happens that experienced shooting athletes, trainers and book writers have slightly different views and terminology. That is normal. Ask if you are not clear on something and find out the reasons behind different opinions. But if we are mistaken about something or the development has simply progressed, make notations directly in your book.

Dear Shooting Sport Athlete

But before you go to bed at night with the book under your pillow, thinking that's how you will win tomorrow, we just want to tell you this on your way to "the top":

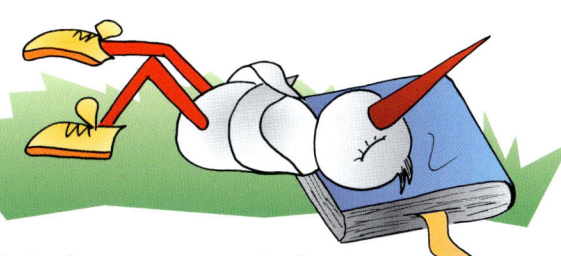

We want to counsel you and explain how you can train properly. But you must train on your own. Whether or not you reach your goal and make it to the peak is mainly up to you.

In this book we primarily offer tips, suggestions and information about training. The section on rifle and pistol shooting describes the basics, but due to limited space it is certainly not complete. Get advice from trainers or other shooting athletes if you need additional information. We hope you have lots of fun with this book. It will certainly provide you with much interesting information to accompany you on a hopefully quick and safe trip to "the summit". We wish you lots of success!

Stork Sammy and the authors

Training Shooting Sports

Sports and Art

Sports and athletes are popular themes for many artists. Many paintings, drawings, caricatures, sculptures, and photographs have been and are created inspired by the elegance of the movement, the beauty of the body, the strength, the fun, and the hi-tech sports equipment. Look for them whenever you are leafing through a magazine or are visiting a public building or a museum.

Logos and mascots

Graphic artists design logos or little mascots for athletic associations, sports clubs or sporting events. These images are then displayed on posters, tickets, trophies, t-shirts, etc., – and of course as plush toys.

Try your hand at graphic design

Pretend your club needs a new logo, or you have to design a medal or the logo for the next World Championships. What do your ideas look like?

...... 2 Interesting Facts About Shooting Sports

Adolescents engage in sports to get in shape, to do something constructive with their free time, to get together with friends and to learn something new and different. Of course you also want to test your limits, push yourself, and be successful in competitions!

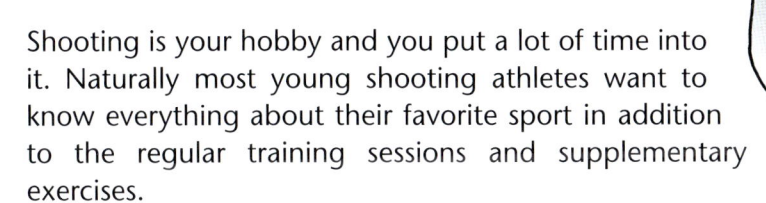

Shooting is your hobby and you put a lot of time into it. Naturally most young shooting athletes want to know everything about their favorite sport in addition to the regular training sessions and supplementary exercises.

That includes learning about the history of shooting sports and national and international shooting sports organizations. You want to know about the various disciplines, the best and most successful athletes and the world records.

That's interesting to you but also to those around you. Some will ask you whether rifle or pistol shooting is actually a sport and what it is you love about it. The more you know about your sport, the more comprehensive and competent your answers will be!

We want to peak your interest within the next few pages. You can get even more information from sport-specific literature, television programs or on the Internet.

Training Shooting Sports

Additional shooting sport disciplines

Crossbow

Shooting a crossbow probably makes most people think of William Tell rather than a modern sport. But since the legendary shot that split the apple, the crossbow has evolved into a piece of hi-tech sports equipment. Most often the transverse arch is mounted on an air rifle stock. Taking aim is similar to rifle shooting, looking through diopter and aperture. Once the bow is cocked, the arrow shaft is placed on a track. When the trigger is pulled, the tension is released and the arrow (or bolt) travels towards the target. We differentiate between sports crossbow and outdoor crossbow.

Shotgun

The special thing about shotgun shooting (as opposed to the other shooting disciplines) is that you shoot at a flying target. You either score a "hit" or "no hit", which the spectators are able to see. Shooting is done with double barrel shotguns, shotgun-pellets are used for ammunition, and the target is a clay disk. We differentiate between three disciplines: trap, double trap and skeet shooting.

Muzzleloaders 25m, 50m and 100m

Permitted are original firearms as long as they meet regulations, and replicas of approved originals. Ammunition is limited to factory-made black powder.

Competitions: percussion rifle, flintlock rifle, flintlock musket, percussion revolver, percussion pistol, flintlock pistol

Event: 15 shots within 40 minutes; beforehand an unlimited number of practice shots within 10 minutes.

Interesting Facts About Shooting Sports

Moving Target 10m

The moving target is fired on at 10 meters standing with an air rifle. The shooter must hold the rifle in the ready position until the moment the target is shown. Only when the target is visible does the shooter move the rifle into firing position and starts to track the target through his sights.

Events: Regular program: low speed (5 sec.) and high speed (2.5 sec.) and a mixed program.

Summer Biathlon

Summer biathlon is a combination of running and shooting, which is what makes this sport so interesting and lends it to audience appeal. Unlike the more well known winter biathlon, the summer biathlete does not carry the rifle while running. During the individual shooting rounds, the shooter must hit five targets with just one shot each. As soon as the target is struck, a flap comes down so everyone can see whether or not the shot was a hit. If the shooter misses a flap, he must run a penalty lap or he has time added to his overall time. From a standing firing position shots are taken on 35mm targets, and from a prone firing position shots are taken on 15mm targets. The equipment consists of a pair of sturdy running shoes, comfortable athletic clothing, as well as a special biathlon air rifle or a small bore target rifle with a five-shot magazine, or regular single-shot rifles.

Events: Relay, Individual, Sprint and Pursuit races.

Training Shooting Sports

Current list of the world's top shooting athletes

It is interesting to keep track of which shooting athletes are the best. Here is a list of important international and national competitions, and you can fill in the blank areas with the names of the current leaders in your favorite disciplines. Use a pencil to record the names and dates so you can always keep your list current.

Competition	Year	Women	Men
Olympic Champion			
World Champion			
European Champion			
US Champion			
State Champion			
Bianchi Cup Team Champions			
Collegiate Team Champions			
National 4-H Invitational Team Champions			

Interesting Facts About Shooting Sports

This is how shooting sports are organized

Organizations for shooting athletes in the United States

USA Shooting (USAS) was chartered by the United States Olympic Committee as the national governing body for the sport of shooting in April 1995. It is headquartered in Colorado Springs, Colorado, at the U.S. Olympic Training Center, and has approximately 5000 members.

Youth shooting athletes

The National 4-H Shooting Sports Foundation works with the International Hunter Education Association (IHEA) and USA Shooting. The focus of this program is the development of youth as individuals by helping them learn to shoot, the safe and responsible use of firearms, and the principles of hunting and archery.

Organisations for shooting athletes in the United Kingdom

The National Small-bore Rifle Association was founded in 1901 and is the National Governing Body for smallbore shooting. It is based at Bisley, Surrey and has a membership of about 6,000 individuals and over 1,000 clubs and associations.

NSRA Olympic disciplines	Other disciplines
Rifle	Crossbow
Pistol	Sporter air rifle

Young Shooters
The NSRA's Youth Proficiency Scheme provides a framework through which young people have the opportunity to take up target shooting. The scheme can be run within a shooting club, but is also used by many youth organisations such as the Scout Association, the Cadet Forces and schools.

To find more information or a club go to www.nsra.co.uk.

Training Shooting Sports

The international association

The international association of shooting athletes is called the **International Shooting Sport Federation (ISSF)**.

The international association of shooting athletes was founded in 1907, as the Union Internationale des Féderations et Associations Nationales de Tir. In 1921, the official name was Union Internationale de Tir (UIT) and since 1998, the official name is International Shooting Sport Federation (ISSF). The ISSF has 158 member associations from 146 countries and is headquartered in Munich, Germany.

If you want to know more, check out the Internet at www.usashooting.com or www.issf-sports.org.

...... 3 Hi There, Petra!

Name: Petra Horneber
Born: April 21, 1965, Floß, Germany

Achievements: 1996 – Olympic silver medal, rifle
1991 and 1993 – World Champion, crossbow 10m
1994 – World Champion small bore-prone
2002 – World Champion small bore-3 x 20
5-time team World Champion, 14 German individual titles

Records:
Olympic record rifle	397 rings
German national record rifle	399 rings
German national record 3 x 20	590 rings
German national record small bore-prone	598 rings

What is so special about your sport?

You are able to directly compare your performance to that of others, regardless of whether it is a shooting athlete from your own club or a world-class shooting athlete. The competition result is a ring number, and I can calculate the difference between that and my own result.

Training Shooting Sports

What must a good shooting athlete be able to do?

It is very important that a shooting athlete be able to control his entire body, deliberately execute individual motion sequences and continue to repeat them right down to the last detail. That requires good body sense and the ability to concentrate for long periods of time. A healthy ambition helps him to perform his training regiment without compromises. A competitive spirit is a good quality for a shooting athlete. A competition does not always go the way one likes or imagines. That's when a good shooting athlete has to take heart and fight to the end.

What were your greatest successes?

My greatest successes weren't all the medals I won! The greatest success of my athletic career was that I became a self-confident person. I am no longer as insecure and fearful as I used to be, and I know now that I have a lot of skills and that I can succeed when I decide to do something.

You were very successful! What were your strong points?

I think I possess all of the physical qualifications of a good shooting athlete. In addition I am very consistent when I have decided to do something. For a long time my sport was at the top of my list and I strictly adhered to my training and preparation regiment. I had lots of support from my family and friends, who never took offense when I arrived at gatherings late or not at all. I also managed to keep my body fit and not partake in and burden my body with the many indulgences of our day and age.

What do you do to keep your body and psyche fit so you can handle those strenuous competitions?

I once had a very bad result on a hot competition day because I had circulation problems in the middle of the competition. That taught me a lesson. I started a strict running program the same day. My psyche also benefited from my absolute consistency.

I prepared for every competition, was able to start at every competition with a positive attitude and therefore had no reason for self-reproach.

Hi There, Petra!

The best method for me was to just accept a loss and immediately look forward again.

How much did you train and was there any time left over for other hobbies?

When I was still active internationally I trained a lot, at least five times a week at the shooting range, and also ran for an hour every other day. That didn't leave much time for other things. But I enjoyed skiing in Winter, which I still like to do. Shooting is now my hobby and I don't train as much as I used to, except of course for competitions.

Do you have a tip for the young shooting athletes?

Enjoy the sport! Always set small goals that you can pursue and achieve. That is how you learn to organize, control and monitor yourself. With these skills you can make it all the way to the top.

Enjoy this great sport!

Petra Horneber

In the future I would like to pass on the experience I have gained in my active years, to other shooting athletes. I am happy for every shooting athlete whose performance I can help improve.

Training Shooting Sports

Fan page

Which shooting athlete would you like to interview?

_____

What would you ask him or her?

_____

_____

_____

_____

_____

Here you can collect autographs or paste photos.

4 Training – the Road to Success

The top shooting athletes stand calmly at the firing range, their aim is steady and the shot hits the center of the target. To score a hit like that would be a dream come true!

Surely you have noticed at practice or at a competition that things don't always go as smoothly as you'd like. You have trouble concentrating, the firearm gets too heavy, you start to wobble and outside noise distracts you…!

You have seen and experienced that others can also shoot pretty well, some even better than you. But what can you do to become a good, and maybe even a top shooting athlete and possibly even a successful member of the national team? One thing is certain: you must train well and often if you want to improve your shooting performance. We would like to help you successfully work toward that goal with this training book.

Don't worry! No one is born a master! The others had to start out like that, too, and only with lots of training did they make it this far.

Training Shooting Sports

The road to the shooting athlete's summit

A training book is no substitute for your trainer, but it can offer you much additional information. Shooting isn't just taking aim and pulling the trigger, but you also need to know about technique, how to improve your fitness level, and about the mental abilities. You have to understand why it is important to also practice other things that don't appear to have anything to do with shooting sports, in addition to shooting at the range.

You should educate yourself about the ideal preparation for training and competition, as well as good nutrition, mental attitude and independent set-up of your safety area at the range.

You think about what you yourself can do at practice and outside of regular training sessions, to improve your performance and to independently monitor and evaluate your progress. Good shooting athletes can do this! After many years of practice and many competitions, they know exactly whether or not they are in shape, how to prepare, what their strengths and weaknesses are, and what they have to work on to get even better.

The trainer is a good friend and advisor to the athletes, but sometimes he also has to be tough when the "inner couch potato" says: "That's too hard today. I quit!"

Training – the Road to Success

Training actively, consciously and systematically

Training in shooting sports means anything you have to do **actively**, **consciously** and **systematically**, to shoot more accurately. But what does that mean?

- **Actively** means you have to do the training yourself. You won't improve by letting the trainer set up and execute the target exercises for you, nor by putting a book on fitness and technique training under your pillow at night. But only by doing the training yourself, i.e. by being active.

- **Consciously** means you understand the purpose and benefits of the exercises the trainer gives you and execute them independently. The young shooting athlete doesn't just do what he is told but also knows why he is doing it. You can even come up with some training exercises of your own, execute them and assign yourself "homework".

- **Systematically** means that you go to practice regularly and learn to work on specific sub-goals within the individual training units. You should keep a record of what you want to do and how you plan to achieve your goals. You can also take notes on the progression of competitions. Not only does it make you feel good but there is also a chance that you will identify deficiencies in your technique, fitness level, or other problems and correct them.

When you know why you are dong something, you will enjoy it more and stick with it longer.

Since a shooting athlete must train many years to achieve a good performance, it makes sense to know right from the start what proper training is and to learn how to train. You will progress more quickly and the training will be much more fun.

Training Shooting Sports

Training correctly – but how?

Prerequisite to training consciously is that you answer a few questions:

- What are my goals?
- What do I want to achieve?
- What is the best way to train?
- Why do I want to train?
- Why am I working so hard?
- How much time do I have for training?
- How often do I have to train?
- What do I need for my training?

For successful athletes, goals are like engines! There are the short-term goals for the next training session or the next competition, and the long-term goals: I want to be World Champion or Olympic Champion some day!

Training – the Road to Success

What do I want to achieve?

In order to train actively and consciously you must have clear goals. If you don't have goals, the training soon won't be fun anymore. Of course you especially want to have fun with shooting sports. But it will only be fun for the long-term if you keep getting a better feel for the firing position, the sights and the timing. A refined technique will help you master the most difficult position, allow you to focus on your shot, let you block out disturbances and adjust to new situations. Or would you be happy always being the weakest one and turn in low ring scores?

Maybe you set a really big goal right away: the World Championships or Olympic shooting events are being shown on television or you watch the major competitions. The shooting athletes are completely focused and technically perfect. Everyone cheers, is amazed and delighted. Now you think: "I want to achieve that, too!"

And that is as it should be! But dreaming of victory is a long way from reality. It will take a lot of sweat, and next to small successes on this road you will also have to accept many defeats.

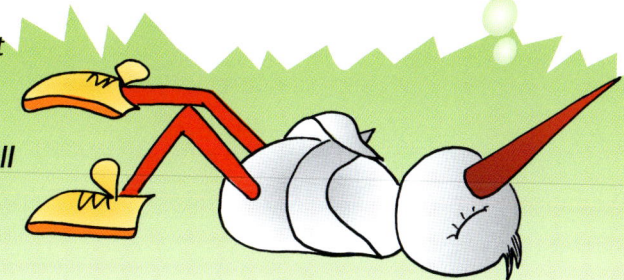

Many goals are still in the distant future but some you can achieve in the short-term. You may decide to perfect your firing position and to cheat less during fitness training. It is fun to reach the goals you have set. And if it doesn't work so well just yet, that can be an incentive.

Don't set goals that are impossible to achieve, but only those you can reach in the near future.

Training Shooting Sports

What I want to achieve	Target date/ I did it!
PP: average 7/10 shots at 25 yards	1.16/ 5.24 ✓
PR: average 8/10 shots at 50 yards	.../...
Juggling three balls for one minute	

Record your goals along with the dates on this chart. In the second column record when you want to reach your goal by. Once you have actually reached it, make a check mark and write the actual date next to it.

Once the chart is full, draw a new one and lay it or paste it in this book. Or you can start a "goal notebook" to use over a longer period of time.

Training – the Road to Success

Doesn't the trainer have to set the goals?

Actually the trainer could determine and set the goals! He could tell you what you could and should achieve. And he will do just that. He sets goals for the training with his athletes, and he designs training plans to use as guidelines for their training and discusses them with his athletes.

But every shooting athlete also knows himself – his strengths and weaknesses – really well. That is why he also knows which goals he can set for himself. It is always better to set your own goals than to have someone else set them for you. You are much more inclined to give everything to achieve them if they are your own goals. If you can tell your trainer exactly what you are having trouble with and what you plan to work harder on in the short term, he can respond to that and help you train.

Of course trainers and athletes sometimes have different points of view. In some cases there is a difference between the goals you want to set for yourself and those the trainer envisions for you. It isn't easy for the trainer. If you think his goals for you are too ambitious, it means he has a lot of confidence in you, but his expectations maybe too high. If you think his goals for you are too low, talk to him and show him that you are capable of more.

Training Shooting Sports

Overall goal and sub-goals

At the last competition, many of Tom's actions were unsuccessful. His firing position got increasingly unstable, his concentration declined during the shooting sequence and the coordination of the technical elements aiming and firing kept getting lost. He is angry but he also realizes what his problem was: a lack of holding strength in legs, trunk, shoulders and arms, the inability to direct his attention, the inability to coordinate the various sub-tasks.

For the next training phase he has decided to work specifically on these performance capacities. That is his overall goal. Of course he can't tackle it all at once and train everything at the same time during the next few training sessions. He has therefore set sub-goals that he can gradually make the focus of his training.

- Create and implement a training plan to improve the stability of his firing position (strengthen leg and core muscles).

- Create and implement a training plan to improve holding strength (shoulders and arm muscles).

- Create and implement a training plan to improve his ability to concentrate (anchoring method).

- Create and implement a training plan to improve coordination with respect to aiming/firing (breathing technique as important control element).

Having occasional successes is good for the motivation – even if at first they are only partial successes!

Training – the Road to Success

hen creating sub-goals it is important to know that the individual abilities and skill levels can also regress when one does not continue to work on them. Meaning the sub-goals that have been achieved are transient, which is why later it becomes important to effectively coordinate the content of the individual training sessions so the various training components do not impede each other and take the overall goal off course.

For example, fitness training should not be scheduled right before technical training. Only a rested body can master subtly coordinated movements at a very high level of concentration for an entire training session. It would be best if you discuss your ideas with your trainer. He will be able to give you some good advice!

Why do I want to train in shooting sports?

The reasons – also called motives – represent the "psychological motor" that initiates the training. They determine whether or not you go to practice, whether you fight or hang your head when you fail. When the weather is bad and you are bored it isn't hard to go to practice. It's a diversion and you get to see your friends and a shooting game really gets you going. But what happens when the sun is shining, when your friends are going to the ice cream parlor or the pool? Maybe there's an interesting show on television? How fast is your gym bag packed then?

Are you still sore because your concentration was so bad the last time you were shooting, or is there still a score to settle with Tom whose high ring score made you feel really insecure? But if you definitely want to reach a sub-goal and you know that the next practice is really important for the lineup at the upcoming competition, then the decision may not be so difficult.

Training Shooting Sports

I go to practice and work hard to achieve top performances

	Very important	Important	Not very important
Because I love the challenge.	☐	☐	☐
Because I want to do something for my health.	☐	☐	☐
Because I want to be a member of a club.	☐	☐	☐
Because my parents want me to.	☐	☐	☐
Because my friend goes, too.	☐	☐	☐
Because I don't want to disappoint my trainer.	☐	☐	☐
Because I like being part of an awesome training group.	☐	☐	☐
Because I don't have anything else to do.	☐	☐	☐
Because you have to be clever for shooting sports.	☐	☐	☐
Because I can concentrate well.	☐	☐	☐
Because I want to get better.	☐	☐	☐
Because I want to have my name in the newspaper.	☐	☐	☐
Because I want to be on the national team some day.	☐	☐	☐
Because shooting sports are just amazing.	☐	☐	☐
Because _____	☐	☐	☐
Because _____	☐	☐	☐

Ask yourself why you want to go to practice and work hard. Decide how important a motive is to you. Make a check mark in the respective column on this list. If you have any additional reasons, add them on the two blank lines.

Training – the Road to Success

What can I do to achieve my goals?

To improve your performance, you should know a few things about training. Then you will better understand why and how you have to do certain exercises. Many sports scientists and doctors have analyzed and researched which training methods are the most beneficial for shooting athletes to achieve top athletic performances and to keep their bodies fit and healthy in spite of the rigorous training. Because just training at random doesn't usually yield the desired results. It can even harm you.

The exertion during training that is supposed to result in an improved performance is called workload. Just as every athlete is different, so are his load-carrying capacity and the workload that is necessary to improve his performance. When an athlete does not exert himself enough during training, he does not achieve a performance increase; and when he exerts himself too much it can lead to exhaustion or physical damage. Unfortunately there is no universal chart the athlete or trainer can look at to see how high the workload should and can be. The athlete has to help with that.

In time he learns to "listen" to his body and to recognize how high his workload needs to be.

What's going on here?

Shhh! Coach, I'm listening for my body to tell me if it can handle a few more exercises!

Training Shooting Sports

Training regularly is important

The correct training workload leads to a performance increase because the body adapts. The heart becomes more efficient, the muscles become stronger and you are able to concentrate for a longer period of time. After training regularly for a while, you notice that you can set up your firing position more easily and hold the firearm more steadily. If you used to be exhausted after a day of competition, you now have more endurance.

But you've most likely already noticed, too, that when you don't train for a while, your "condition" declines. At your first practice after the break, the motion sequences and exercises seemed more difficult and your performance was not as good. So you had to start over with a lower workload than what you finished your last training session with.

Do you remember our example about the summit you are trying to reach? Laziness and training interruptions disrupt performance development. You are thrown backward a ways on the road to success. It is as if you slid back a little on the path you already climbed.

Even on vacation there are many opportunities to stay in shape. Go jogging, do some strength exercises, stretch in your room or work on your agility. Use the Summer to work on your strength and endurance by swimming, jogging, skating or mountain biking. You can ski in Winter. It will make catching up after vacation a little easier.

Training – the Road to Success

What makes someone a good shooting athlete?

Surely you can think of many good answers to this question. There is much a good shooting athlete must have, know and be able to do. On this chart we attempt to illustrate everything that impacts the performance of a shooting athlete and what has to be trained. The individual factors are always connected. That is why in the illustration the circles also overlap. The circle of mental abilities surrounds everything because they affect everything. In addition there are important exterior influences, which you can see on the outer arrows.

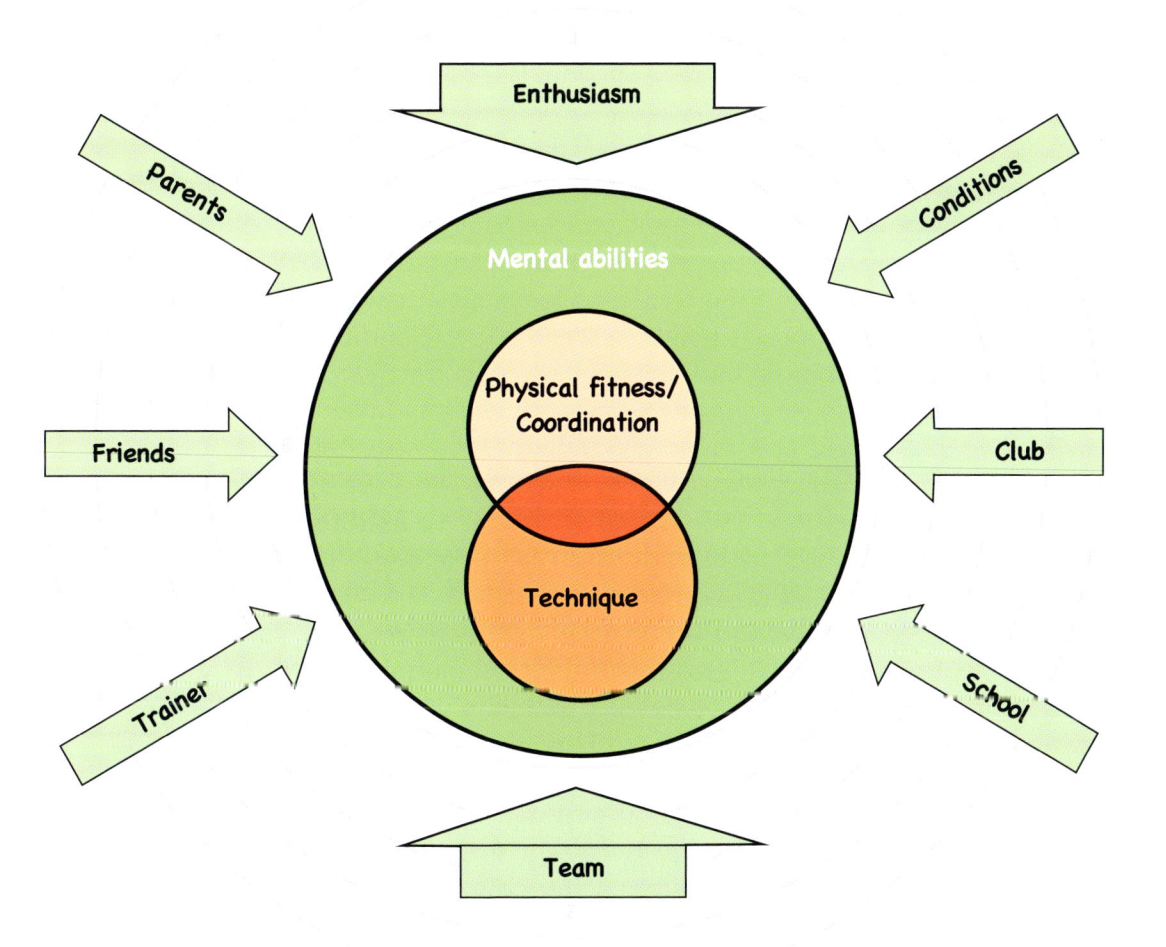

Training Shooting Sports

A shooting athlete who has good **physical fitness** and is strong is said to have a high fitness level. In a competition you want to have a stable firing position, be able to raise and hold your firearm over and over again as well as stay completely focused. To do so you have to be totally fit for the entire competition and season.

Technique refers to the specific motion sequences in shooting sports. These include getting set up, settling into firing position, and the technical elements aiming, firing, follow-through and breathing.

The **psyche** determines how confident, determined or timid you are, whether a missed shot discourages or spurs you on to fight all the more. A shooting athlete must learn to fully concentrate on the target, to focus his attention on the important points in the sequence, and to control his excitement by breathing correctly.

Our chart also shows arrows like **parents, friends, trainer, conditions, club and school**. (You could certainly add more). All of these are outside influences that affect the performance of the shooting athlete. Whether or not your parents understand you and support your training is very important. How well you get along with your trainer and teammates is also relevant. Problems at school, conflict with friends or family stress do not allow for a clear head. What's great is when the training conditions are ideal and you get the necessary support. But without the necessary **enthusiasm** you won't be likely to achieve top performances.

Training – the Road to Success

All of the factors combined spell success

Shooting sports are highly demanding in terms of endurance, strength and flexibility. That is why physical fitness is so important. But being fit alone does not make you a successful shooting athlete. You also need coordination, great technique and smart tactics. But you only become really good when, in addition to these abilities, you also acquire good mental qualifications.

What does that mean for your training?

The most important training is certainly done at the shooting range. There you can train nearly all of the essential elements: you have to hold the firearm steady, demonstrate nerves of steel, and experiment to see which technique is most successful. Someone who practices a lot has the best chance of making progress in training. But if you notice specific weaknesses in your field then it's time for some additional specialized training. In the following chapters we will explain the individual factors in more detail and talk about training methods. We will show you opportunities for practicing at home, for self-monitoring and evaluation of your own performance. Also discuss everything with your trainer. He knows the ropes.

Awesome, Julie! I'm excited! You just shot another amazing series!

But Coach, that's a no-brainer! We have a fancy shooting range, new firearms, and my parents are rooting for me!

Yesterday I got the best report card of my life and I made up with my friend Tina!

Besides, I'm in love! Any more questions?

Training Shooting Sports

Training diary

Every shooting athlete should keep a diary. In this book you record training content, training goals, competition dates, results, shot patterns, evaluations and your personal settings for sports equipment and gear. Write down your long-term and short-term training goals and assess how you can achieve them and what you plan to do next. A precise competition plan is important so you can make specific preparations.

- Annual plan
- Monthly plan
- Weekly plan
- Training log
- Competition log
- Personal records

Also, plan your supplementary training, such as jogging, cycling, strength training, coordination exercises, etc. By the way: someone who sets his own goals is also subject to a self-imposed "goal award" or, when necessary, additional exercises!

38

Physical Fitness and Coordination

. . . 5 Physical Fitness and Coordination

An outsider may think that shooting sports are all about a good eye and accurate aiming. Maybe you have heard the argument that shooting isn't a real sport since there is barely any movement! Of course you know very well how fit a shooting athlete has to be to perform well in training and at competitions.

That is why in this chapter you will find lots of information on the subject of physical fitness. Someone who is in good physical condition is better able to handle physiological stress.

Settling into firing position, a stable stance and holding the equipment steady require the shooting athlete to possess a high degree of body control. That's the only way to not just score accidental 10 s, but entire series of successful hits.

In this chapter we have described and compiled general information on physical fitness that is particularly important for shooting athletes. And there are also many exercises and fitness tips.

Even if it isn't very apparent from the outside, there are many muscles involved in shooting!

39

Training Shooting Sports

How fit are you?

How would you rate your physical fitness level? Here we have listed a few requirements, and you can choose between the smiley faces and make a check mark!

Fitness-related requirements	😊	😐	☹
Sustained jogging, cycling, swimming or ball sports …			
Fast sprint, jumping, throwing …			
Push-ups, sit-ups, pull-ups …			
Balancing on a narrow beam or bench, Standing and hopping on one leg …			
Flexibility, like head twists and hip twists …			
Reacting quickly to light signals, sound or touch …			
Keen vision and recognition of objects near and far …			
Volleying sports, like ping-pong, tennis, squash, badminton, volleyball …			
Aiming games, like darts, billiards, bowling, nine pins …			

Defining physical fitness

In sports the term fitness refers foremost to someone's *physical abilities*. Your fitness level determines how much endurance you have and how fast you are, how much strength you have and how agile you are. For example, you can tell how fit you are by how quickly you get winded after a quick sprint, how long you can tolerate athletic exertion without getting really sore, how powerful your sprints are and how high you can jump.

Your fitness level will improve with regular training, but also by doing other sports.

The fitness-related abilities

We would now like to give a more detailed explanation of the most important fitness-related abilities a shooting athlete must have to be in all-around good shape. They include:

- Endurance
- Strength
- Speed
- Flexibility

Training Shooting Sports

Endurance

Endurance is the necessary prerequisite for handling exertion over an extended period of time. That includes not getting tired too quickly during strenuous training, a competition or, for instance, while traveling to a competition. Your body should be able to recover quickly after a relatively major exertion. This is called *regeneration*.

That means someone who has good endurance is physically fit, recovers quickly after training or a competition and is able to concentrate for a longer period of time.

A great deal is demanded from a shooting athlete at a competition. He must have good endurance so he can compete with full concentration and in the best physical condition, without getting continuously weaker and more fatigued.

How can you train for endurance?

Training at the shooting range always includes an endurance segment. Next to the necessary exertion it can also be a lot of fun. Athletic games are particularly well suited for a group setting.

Basic endurance is developed primarily through endurance running. You should run at least two to three times a week for 20 minutes. Swimming, biking, power walking, skating or skiing are also good choices. Together with your friends you can play soccer, volleyball, team handball, streetball or beach volleyball.

Physical Fitness and Coordination

Strength

Strength is necessary when you want to move something heavy like lifting, thrusting, pulling or pushing weights. Without strength you cannot execute movements, particularly athletic movements. You also need strength to hold your body or parts of your body in a particular position, to move quickly or to slow down movement.

As a shooting athlete you need lots of strength in your hands, arms and shoulders to hold your sports equipment, as well as in your core and legs for a stable, well-balanced firing position.

Sports strength can be divided into different types:

Maximum strength: The most strength you can possibly muster *(powerlifting, working out with weights).*
Power: You can convert strength as quickly as possible *(throwing contest, shot put, high jump).*
Endurance strength: You can maintain the exertion over an extended period of time *(push-ups, sit-ups, mountain biking, downhill skiing, … holding a pistol or rifle).*

Never strengthen just one muscle, but always pay attention to the antagonist, the "opposing player".

The illustration shows the "muscle man" with a bent arm. Responsible for this bending is the flexor, the biceps. That is the muscle that contracts when you want to show someone "your muscles". The extensor, the triceps is responsible for the extension of the arm.

Feel your muscles! If you push down on a tabletop with your hand, the triceps gets hard because it wants to extend the arm in the elbow. The biceps is soft because it is relaxed and yields. But if you push against the table from below, the biceps is hard and the triceps is soft.

43

Training Shooting Sports

Exercises for a strong core

A stable firing position requires particularly strong abdominal and back muscles. Here we have listed various exercises you should do regularly.

- Before you do the exercises, get warmed up by jogging, playing ball games and stretching!
- Perform the stretches slowly and gently!
- Do them in 3-4 sets with 10-20 repetitions each!
- Don't forget to breathe!

1 Vertical back muscles

Lie on your back. Now lift your head and your legs off the floor and carefully draw your knees to your forehead.

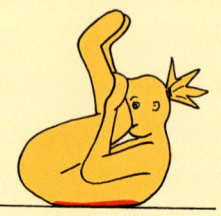

2 Exterior oblique muscles

Sit tall on a chair and hold a staff or a cord overhead with your elbows bent. Now slowly twist your trunk from side to side.

3 Upper back and shoulder muscles

Lie on your stomach with your hands at your sides. Now lift both arms to the front, at the same time lift head and shoulders off the floor. Hold it for approx. two seconds and slowly return to the floor.

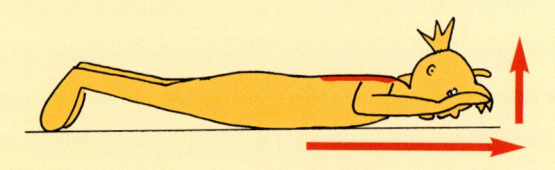

Physical Fitness and Coordination

4 Back and abdominal muscles

Lie on your back and slowly lift head, shoulders and bent knees off the floor. Now imagine you are in a rowboat and perform the rowing motion. The legs are not fully extended.

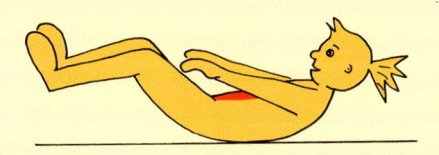

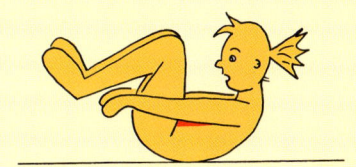

5 Gluteal and back muscles

Lie on your stomach with arms and legs extended. Now alternately "pump" both arms and legs up and down.

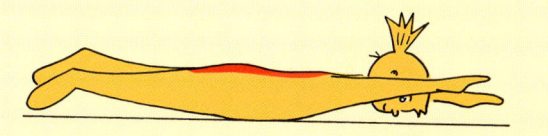

6 Gluteal and back muscles

Get on your hands and knees keeping your elbows slightly bent. Now extend the right leg and the left arm until both are horizontal – swimmer!

Now roll up into a ball and bring the knee to the forehead – stool! After 10 repetitions switch sides!

A strong core requires all around strong muscles – back, abdominals, gluteals! That is why your training must be well balanced!

You can find additional exercises in our previous book "Learning Shooting Sports".

Training Shooting Sports

Speed

Speed is the ability you need to execute a movement with the greatest possible acceleration and velocity. The rather static shooting sports do not require maximum velocity like sprinting, ball sports or swimming. But in some of the shooting sports disciplines (duel, rapid fire, shotgun) the athlete needs good reaction speed and speed of movement.

In sports we differentiate between:

Reaction speed: As a shooting athlete you must be able to quickly react to specific visual stimuli (i.e. a target).

Speed of movement: You are able to execute the necessary movement or the required technique as fast as demanded.

How can you train for speed?

Speed can be trained along with endurance and strength training. While training at the shooting range, make sure that you train at the correct speed as soon as you have mastered the motion sequence. Your trainer will tell you how long a shot sequence should take.

Good options away from the shooting range are all other ball games, relays and catching games that require quick movements and lightning-fast reaction. Playing reaction games is also great practice.

Physical Fitness and Coordination

Agility

This is often also referred to as flexibility. It is apparent in how far an athlete is able to flex and extend his joints, to what extent his tendons, muscles and ligaments will tolerate a movement. Of course this also has something to do with your age, build, strength and coordination, and the elasticity of your muscles and tendons. But it is primarily a matter of training.

Muscles and tendons must adapt to the special positions and movements in shooting sports. This includes the ideal position of head, shoulders, hips and feet. You want to assume a stable stance to concentrate on aiming and firing without major fluctuations.

How can you train for agility?

There are numerous exercises for increasing the flexibility of all joints from head to toe. You can also find some of them in this book.

But before you demonstrate your agility and begin with the exercises, don't forget to warm up. Vigorous stretching of cold muscles and tendons can lead to injuries.

WHAT IS GOING ON WITH YOU?

BUT COACH, WE ARE SUPPOSED TO SHOW HOW AGILE WE ARE!

47

Training Shooting Sports

Reaction exercises

These exercises will teach you to recognize the right moment and react quick as lightning. A suitable exercise partner is anyone who thinks it's fun: friends, parents, grandparents, siblings, etc.

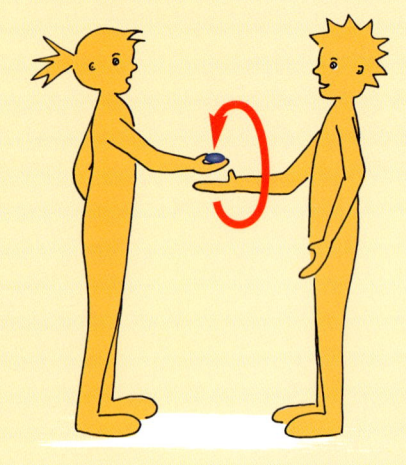

1 Snatch the coin

One partner holds the coin or some other small object in the open palm. You hold your hand underneath his and try to find the perfect moment to suddenly snatch the coin. The partner can quickly pull his hand away.

2 Catch the staff

Your partner holds a staff or similar object in his hand. You stand facing him. Now he will suddenly release the object and you must quickly catch it so it doesn't drop to the ground.

3 Catch the hand

Your partner stands as shown in the illustration. His hands are held about 8 inches apart and now you must try to move your hand through this gap. He will clap his hands together to catch yours.

Try to move your hand at varying speeds to mislead and outfox your partner.

Try the following and you will be amazed: Start by moving your hand really fast and then stop before you get to his hands. Of course he will clap his hands together. When he opens them again, slowly slide your hand through.

Physical Fitness and Coordination

Reaction games

Games of skill are a great way to bridge boring waiting time. Just be careful not to get in the way of other people or traffic.

1 Touch the knee

You stand facing your partner and both of you try to touch the other's knee with your hand. At the same time you have to protect your own knee by dodging him. You can even form teams.

2 Step on the feet

Stand across from your partner and hold each other's hands. Now try to step on each other's toes. Be careful not to step on your own feet. This is about skill and not about hurting your partner!

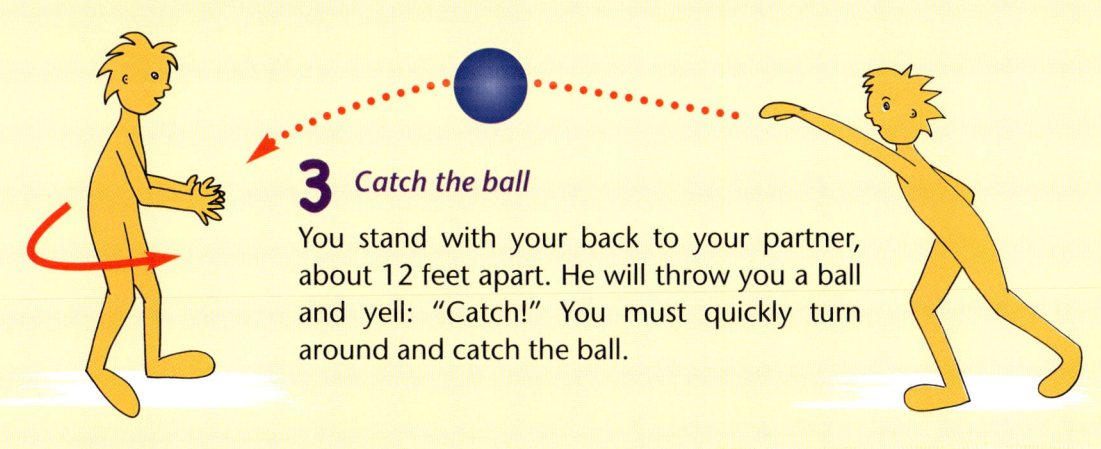

3 Catch the ball

You stand with your back to your partner, about 12 feet apart. He will throw you a ball and yell: "Catch!" You must quickly turn around and catch the ball.

4 Stick side to side

One partner constantly stays at the right or left side of the other. The other partner tries to shake him off by walking, running or turning. (No spinning in a circle!) Let's see who can manage to hang on the longest!

The object of all games is quick reaction and fast movement!

Training Shooting Sports

Agility exercises

Don't forget: Don't start the exercises until after you have warmed up! Before a workout you should only limber up (stretch lightly) and after the workout stretch more vigorously.

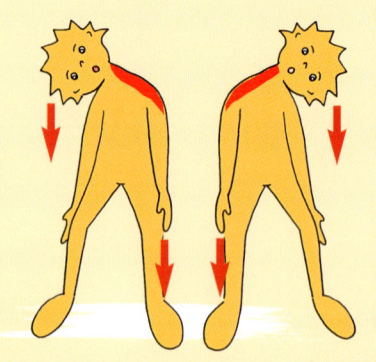

1 Stretching the neck muscles

Stand with your legs slightly apart and bend your head to one side. Then switch sides. Now turn your head far to the right and then to the left side.

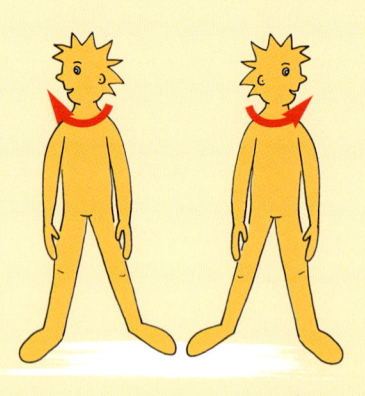

2 Stretching shoulder, back and arm muscles

- With your free hand grasp your shoulder or elbow and pull the arm back.
- For the second exercise, the arm is behind the head and you push the elbow toward the floor.

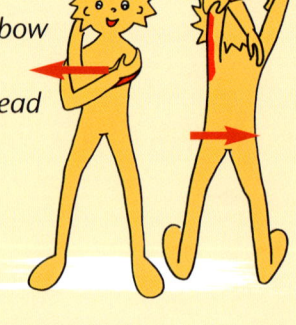

3 Stretching chest, back and shoulder muscles

The upper body folds forward and the hands rest on a banister, the back of a chair or a table. Now press your upper body down further.

4 Stretching the back

Sit back on your heels. Your feet are extended. Now extend your arms forward on the floor and relax.

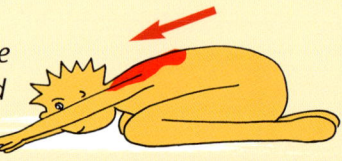

Physical Fitness and Coordination

5 Stretching the lower back

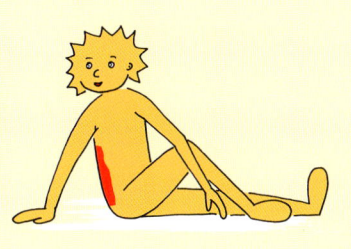

In a sitting position, bend the right knee and keep the left leg extended forward. The left arm gently presses again the outside of the bent leg. At the same time the upper body and head slowly rotate to the right. Then switch sides!

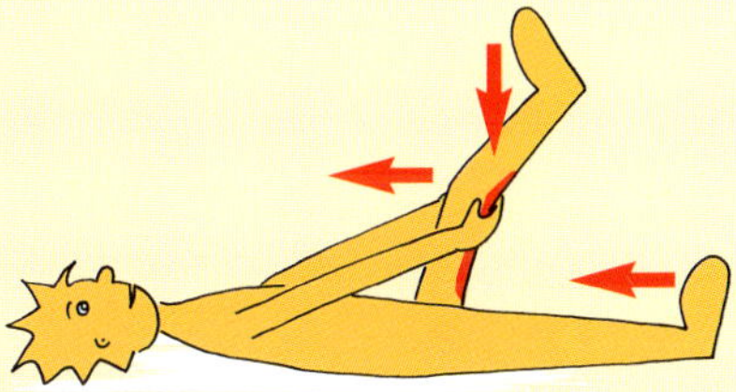

6 Stretching the hamstring

Lie on the floor and grasp the extended leg with both hands and pull the knee toward the chest. The other leg remains extended on the floor. Now extend the leg slowly and flex both feet.

7 Stretching the hip muscles

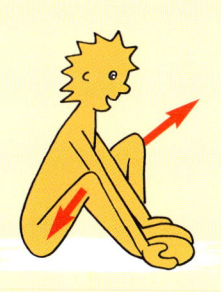

Sit upright and bring the soles of your feet together and hold them close to your body. Slowly open your knees. Now press with your elbows against the inside of your knees to open them further.

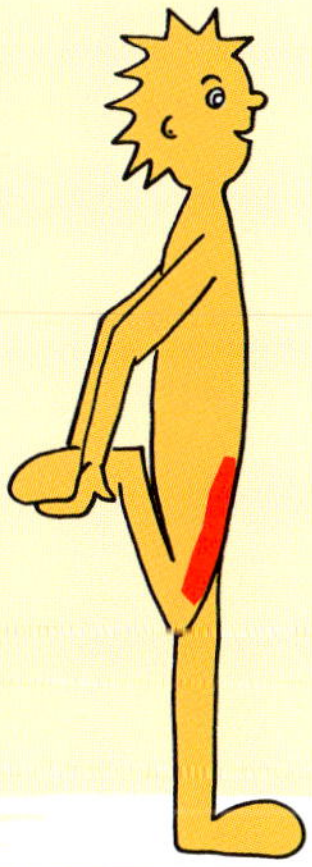

8 Stretching the quadriceps

From a standing position, bend one leg back. Now gently pull at the ankle. The hip remains straight and the knees stay together. For better balance you can place one hand against the wall.

Hold each stretch for at least 10 seconds. Slowly increase the stretch until you feel a slight pull, but it should not hurt! You can find many additional exercises in a variety of books and magazines.

Training Shooting Sports

Coordination

Shooting sports require good coordination. A well-balanced interplay between all of the participating muscles and the nervous system is very important for the individual movements. That means that the necessary amount of endurance, strength, speed and agility must be balanced for each shooting discipline.

In shooting sports we differentiate between different coordinative abilities. There are many options for training your coordinative abilities, at home or outdoors.

Balance

Once you have settled into firing position you try not to allow any wobbles. Every sway results in a deviation from the target!

Standing on one leg, balancing, riding a unicycle, dry runs (also without shoes) on thick mats or balance pads.

Sense of rhythm

The shooting movements are always subject to a certain rhythm. This makes settling into firing position, aiming and firing much easier. Especially when you have to fire several shots in a row, a specific rhythm in the sequence is necessary.

Shot rhythm training and shooting rhythm training with a stopwatch, with and without commands from the trainer.

Reaction ability

It is the ability to identify the correct sight picture and fire on it.

Catching games, reaction games, target training, mounted on a white disc/on a mirror disc.

Physical Fitness and Coordination

Linking ability

As the word suggests, the movements are linked together. These are movements and tactical sequences in shooting sports that occur simultaneously or in immediate succession.

> Element training: Holding, breathing, aiming, firing, practiced individually.
> Combination training: Holding – breathing – holding – aiming, aiming – firing, practice entire sequence.

Differentiation ability

A shooting athlete must have the ability to correctly gage speed, exertion and distance. This is important for sensible movement, accurate aim, precise firing and sufficient follow-through/maintaining position.

> Ball toss with different size targets/varying distances, balloon tag, shooting at small/large discs, shooting with more/less trigger pull, shooting with/without loading, left-handed firing position for right-handers.

Orientation ability

You must have the ability to continuously orientate yourself in the surrounding space with each movement and to quickly align yourself to the target.

> Locate people blindfolded by sound, ball games, at the shooting range: set up – blind firing position – check zero point – start from the beginning.

Adaptation and reorientation ability

Of course you hope for quiet, ideal light conditions and no disturbances or delays at the shooting range. But conditions are not always ideal! It is important to quickly adapt to a new situation.

> Several athletes each juggle a balloon and at the same time attempt to swat away the balloon of another, training with disturbances, changeable light conditions, cold/heat.

Training Shooting Sports

Coordination exercises

We explained coordinative abilities on the previous pages and the following are our exercise suggestions.

1 Rhythmic hopping

- Hop along a line in an even rhythm and make a quarter turn with each hop.
- Draw a serpentine on the floor and try to hop along the line with both feet in an even rhythm.

2 With eyes closed

Stand tall with your eyes closed.
- Extend your arms to the side.
- Extend your arms overhead.
- Step into a forward lunge/side lunge, and back.

3 Stand on one leg

- Switch legs – first right, then left.
- At the same time, close your eyes.
- Extend your arms to the side and then overhead.

4 Stand on a wobbly surface

- Stand on a mat, a pillow or a rolled up blanket.
- Stand on a narrow log.
- Stand on a core board or a gyro exerciser.

Physical Fitness and Coordination

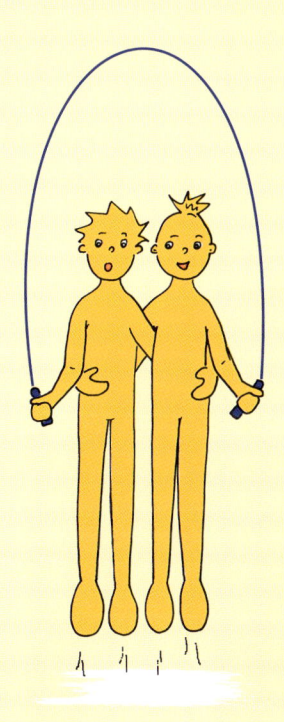

5 Jump rope

- Modify as you jump: hop between jumps, double under jumps, walking, arms crossed, etc...
- Partner jumping in tandem or side-by-side.

6 Duel

Stand back to back with a partner. Who will win the "pushing duel"?

7 Juggling

Juggling with balls or other suitable objects is a very good exercise. It is a great way to train eye to hand coordination.

8 Games of patience

Watch out! This is no child's play!

Building a tower on a wobbly surface, playing "Jenga" or similar games of patience requires a good eye and especially a steady hand.

Surely you can think of even more exercises to train your coordinative abilities.

Training Shooting Sports

. . . 6 It's All in the Mind

Why is it that humans can feel joy and sadness, that they can fall in love or hate someone? Why are people able to think, remember and dream?

People have always been curious about what goes on inside our bodies. No one had an explanation, so they called the whole thing the soul. The famous physician Rudolf Virchow (1821-1902) once asked his students to find the souls in the human body. But what they found inside the bodies they dissected was the brain, the heart, the lungs, the liver, and all of the other organs. But they did not find a soul.

Of course they could not have found it, because our ability to perceive and imagine, to think and decide, and to feel and want are the result of our brain's activity. The science that deals with this is called *psychology*, and the old term *soul* was replaced by the word *psyche*.

Thus mental, or psychological abilities, refers to the shooting athlete's ability to handle joy, anger, rage, excitement, competitiveness, fear and the many other emotions, and to advantageously and successfully apply them in training and during competitions. In psychology, research is also being done on how the thinking process works and how our muscles receive commands. We imagine our brain as a computer that controls everything. While you are shooting, your "computer" is working at high capacity, which is why its programs must be well synchronized.

Training Shooting Sports

Perception

A good shot is only possible if the shooter can quickly perceive and correctly process important information. In shooting sports the object is primarily to completely and accurately apprehend the modules of the target in fractions of seconds, and to sense the motion, pressure and strength in the muscles. You react at just the right moment to release the shot.

Perception – Control – Brain – Muscle

The illustrations show a simplified version of how this process works. You receive lots of information via receptors located in our sensory organs. You can see, hear, taste and feel something. Nerve tracts then carry this information to the brain. On the way to the brain the information first ends up at a circuit. In our illustration this is a piece of bone marrow located in the spinal column. The brain then sends an "order" to the respective muscle, telling it what to do.

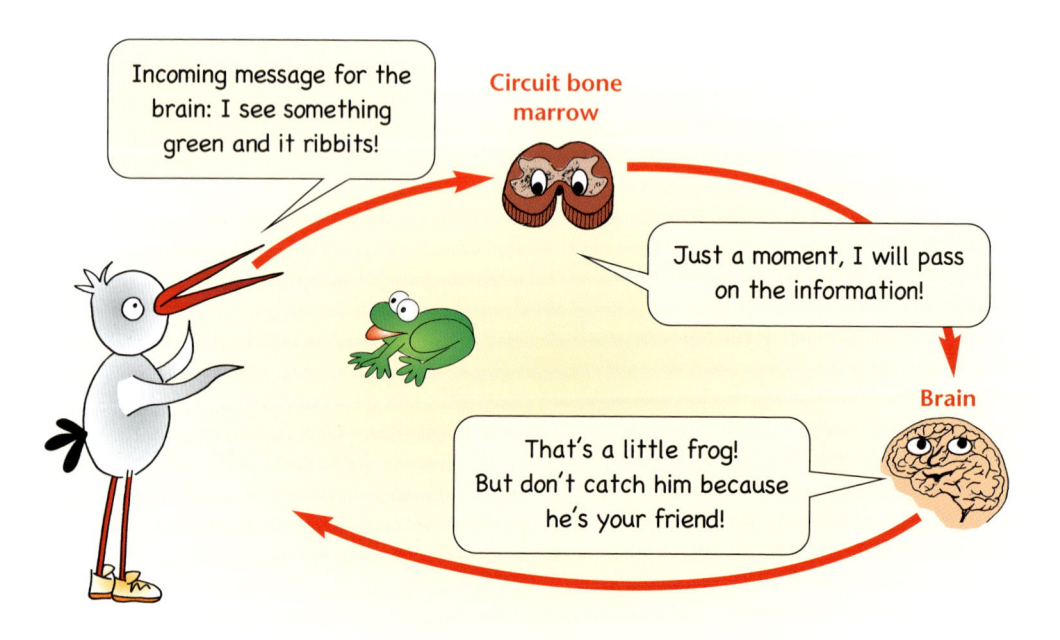

Visual discrimination

Distinguishing the sight picture – rear sight/diopter, front sight/aperture, light bars, bull's eye, etc. – is critical to a good shot. Accurate assessment of the target requires a huge differentiation effort by the shooter. Even minor visual errors result in differences of whole ring numbers.

In technical jargon this is referred to as visual discrimination ability. The eye plays the leading role while the brain makes the decisions.

Delicate and sensitive

Shooting sports require a well-developed sense of movement and pressure sensitivity. Your sensors work very accurately during small and delicate movement tasks. A clean trigger pull is very challenging, and in shooting sports is the pivotal task. It must be timed with the sight picture.

Directing successful motion sequences in shooting sports requires good body control and a lot of feeling!

Reaction

Reacting quickly, correctly and accurately is a very important requirement for a shooting athlete. The shooter must react immediately to the correct sight picture as well as modifications and disruptions, with the appropriate action.

We differentiate between reactions to a suddenly occurring signal (sight picture appears during the aiming process) and the reaction to an anticipated signal (e.g., during rapid fire or duel shooting).

Training Shooting Sports

How you feel, meaning your state of mind has a major impact on your athletic performance. Mostly it is up to you whether you are in a positive or negative mood. You can influence your frame of mind with thoughts, by talking to yourself or through self-instruction.

Attitude with negative impact

You don't feel well physically, you don't like the conditions at the shooting range and the warm-up wasn't very encouraging. You think it's going downhill from here. And with that attitude it probably will!

- *Unfavorable external conditions*
  "I'll never perform well in these light conditions! That alwayshappens!"

- *Bad shot*
  "Now I've started with an 8 again, but I absolutely have to shoot a 10!"

- *The previous results weren't phenomenal*
  "Why am I even here? When I think about my previous results I know I don't even have a chance!"

- *Bad start of competition*
  "I'm a loser! Everyone laughed at me. I should just go home!"

- *Good start of competition*
  "Oh well, I guess I got lucky! Every dog has his day!"

It's All in the Mind

Be open to encouragement! The trainer, friends and parents comfort you, they listen when you doubt yourself, give you advice or even distract you!

Attitude with positive impact

You believe in yourself, you take heart and spur yourself on. You recognize the advantages in the external conditions and think about successful competitions. With this attitude you can't but succeed! Spur yourself on without getting inattentive or boastful.

- *Unfavorable external conditions*
  "No problem, it's a chance to try out my technical strengths!"

- *Bad shot*
  "It happens, but now I'll concentrate on getting a clean shot!"

- *The last results weren't phenomenal*
  "I trained diligently but the results weren't great. But now it's time! Today is the day!"

- *Bad start of competition*
  "It happens, no problem! I'll make it up! I'll show them!"

- *Good start of competition*
  "What do you know – today is great! If I don't lose my focus now it will continue to go well!"

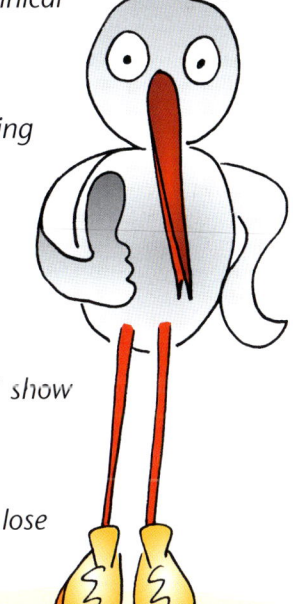

Training Shooting Sports

Mental state

You prepare for a tournament by training a lot. You continuously work on your technique and tweak your firing position. You get tips, correct mistakes and practice until you've got it. You have an amazing series. Now you are totally prepared and just have to do everything like you do at practice. But what's going on? You are shaking with anxiety; you can't get the mark in your sights and pull the trigger too soon. You can barely concentrate on the target. Are you now hopelessly at the mercy of your feelings and your trembling legs, or can the psyche be trained as well? We assure you that there is something you can do!

First of all it is very important to know exactly what is going on inside of you. When you know the causes you can adapt yourself more easily and prepare for such situations.

Tension and nervousness

Nervousness before a competition is normal and important. No athlete can be successful if he is totally relaxed and laid back about everything. This inner tension helps you to perform at your best. Only, too much anxiety is bad. You cannot concentrate as well, are stiff and – most importantly – you make mistakes.

Fear

There are different reasons why an athlete maybe afraid. Sometimes it is fear of reacting badly and failing. Also, the handling of special pieces of sports equipment that requires you to observe specific safety regulations can be scary. For some there may be the fear of pulling the trigger. Maybe you had some bad results recently or you are not sure you are good enough for your team? Or maybe you are being criticized?

A little respect is very useful. It makes you more serious, focused and vigilant. Otherwise a fearful shooter will be unsure of himself and will lack the necessary willpower. You can combat that negative feeling

It's All in the Mind

through training, by talking to your teammates, your trainer, your parents or friends. Relaxation exercises are often helpful, as well as competition-specific training and goal-directed training.

Anger

You can be angry at many things – your trainer, your teammates, your parents, your friend, the opponent, school, etc. Maybe the technique isn't working as well at practice or in a competition as you had anticipated. Or are you sometimes angry about "bad" equipment or poor lighting? You must learn to deal with aggressive feelings. Don't make your equipment, trainer or teammate the focus of your anger. If you feel angry, use that feeling to bring even more focus to the task at hand. Stay calm and use it as an incentive.

Talking to yourself a little can often help with your concentration, give you courage and spur you on!

My opponents will be amazed! I can do this!

Stay calm in firing position! I'm as solid as a rock!

I'm completely calm and all sensors are activated!

Awesome! That was my second 10! Keep it up!

It's working! Now just stay focused!

I got distracted for a moment! Now focus only on the next shot!

Alright! Another awesome hit! Today is my day!

Training Shooting Sports

Perseverance

As a shooting athlete you will always find yourself in situations where you are anxious, afraid or angry, where you push yourself to the limit or are just plain unenthusiastic. You should be able to tough it out at practice, get better and, when necessary, grit your teeth and bear it. Always look for new challenges and be ready to try something new. You will meet your limits time and again, and learn to push past them in a sensible way.

Such challenges may include:

- *Fear of strong opponents.*
  "I can't catch up with him. He's too strong!"

- *Limited physical capacity in training.*
- "I can't go on, it is too strenuous! I can't concentrate anymore and my arm is so heavy!"

- *Fear of new things.*
- "I've never used this firearm before! Why am I supposed to try something new right now? I'm sure it won't work out!"

- *Conflict with trainers or training buddies*
  "It's always my fault! No one notices my difficulties! No one helps me! No one likes me!"

Get over your fears and you will be proud of yourself later. Perseverance in sports toughens you up and also helps you cope with problems at school and in other areas of your life.

If you're not sure how to handle problems, get some advice. Surely your parents, trainer, friends or your doctor are people you can talk to.

It's All in the Mind

Alertness and the ability to concentrate

Whether there is commotion at the shooting range just now, people are calling out, or your opponent is happy about a great shooting score – don't get distracted! You must be completely focused on your mark. Thinking about private issues, fear of possible mistakes or losing is distracting. Problems at school or what to wear to the next party should also be disregarded during practice or a competition.

Tips for improving attentiveness

◉ **Focus completely on your mark!**
When you don't really feel like concentrating on a task anymore, every little thing will distract you. You think about what your friends are doing or watch a bird fly past. Plan to focus briefly but completely on just one task at a time. That can be a shot sequence at practice or a school assignment. It will definitely save time and energy!

◉ **Don't get distracted!**
During training, concentrate in turn on the individual subcomponents of your entire sequence, and after every shot mentally start over from the beginning. If instead you look to see what the spectators are doing, you will direct attention away from the shooting sequence, and if you then think about what would happen if you made a mistake, it's already done!

◉ **Take a concentration break!**
Your ability to concentrate is not endless. Every person has to rest and also restore his mental strength! During the shooting sequence, focus your attention specifically on the sub-steps and mentally "put it into neutral" between shots and simply observe your ritual actions, e.g. setting down the firearm, picking up the firearm, loading, changing the target, etc.

The skill in shooting lies in mentally being at the right place at the right time and the ability to "tune out" between shot sequences without getting distracted!

Training Shooting Sports

Pressure is caused by expectations

Has it happened to you that you failed at a competition in spite of perfect preparation and very good training results? Everyone was astonished and you were stunned. What went wrong? What happened to you is the same thing that can happen to very successful athletes at important competitions. The pressure was too much! You were too anxious, couldn't concentrate and weren't able to deliver your actual performance.

Depending on the importance of the competition, this can be very aggravating. You need to know why something like this happens and what you can do about it.

- Pressure comes from **external expectations**. They come from your parents, your trainer, the club and your friends. They expect (or so you think) you to perform well.

- And then there are your own expectations for yourself. You set personal goals that you want to achieve.

I want to be good!
Show us what you can do!
We are counting on you!
Don't make any mistakes!
I'm really going to bring it!
My trainer will be amazed!
I want to score lots of points today!
We're proud of you!
I'm going to show them all!

Sometimes this performance pressure gets to be too much. You become afraid of not being able to meet the high expectations of others or yourself. And that's stressful!

It's All in the Mind

How to deal with pressure

- **Get well prepared for the competition at practice during the week.** Train diligently and with concentration. Prepare yourself properly for the demands that await you. Then nothing that happens will be a surprise.

- **Get everything ready the night before,** double check everything, go to bed early, eat a good breakfast and leave your house on time.

- **Leave behind any problems** that have nothing to do with the competition. Imagine that no other problems can touch you once you're at the shooting range. You concentrate only on the competition and the mark. You need to have so called tunnel vision.

- **When you set goals for yourself, you also choose the pressure you will be under.** Of course you could also set goals that are easier to reach and avoid the pressure by, for instance, not wanting to win anyway or by not even competing at all. Set high but realistic goals for yourself. A little pressure is necessary. It's fun, spurs you on and is the only way to deliver a good performance.

- **Pressure builds character!** You will only get strong and more resilient every time if you continue to handle pressure situations. Someone who already avoids pressure and constantly makes excuses will become a "weakling", and will always fall short of his potential. Conquering your fears will strengthen your character.

Watch successful shooting athletes as they relax and concentrate at the shooting stand and during breaks. How do they react to mistakes, a change in the situation, successes and defeats? Try to emulate them and find out what works best for you. Practice these rituals and carry them out again and again. Character traits you develop in shooting sports will also be useful in other areas of life!

Training Shooting Sports

Relax with yoga

This centuries old Indian practice focuses on the harmony between body, spirit and soul. It includes breathing exercises and physical exercises to slowly stretch muscles and ligaments. You connect with your inner self, find your center, become more relaxed and focused.

Corpse pose

Lie flat on your back, completely relaxed, on a not too soft surface. The arms rest along side the body, the palms face upward and the eyes are closed. Try to relax all of your muscles, empty your mind, don't worry about anything, and don't plan anything! Breathe gently and slowly. "Go deaf" if thoughts try to interfere!

Mountain pose

You stand firm and tall on the earth like a mountain. The head is erect, the shoulders are relaxed and the arms hang at your sides. When you close your eyes it becomes more difficult to keep your balance. Imagine a vertical line running from your head to your toes. Focus on this!

Breathing

Your breath should flow slowly and evenly. You feel how good inhaling is for you and how you exhale everything that is unpleasant. You become mentally balanced and fill up with new energy.

You can practice belly breathing, chest breathing and alternate nostril breathing as you relax in corpse pose, mountain pose or sitting lotus. Lay your hands on your stomach or chest to feel the inhalations and exhalations.

Breathe evenly during all exercises! Never hold your breath!

It's All in the Mind

Salutation

The salutation is a flowing movement in which the hands are brought together overhead. This exercise is very good for breathing because the extended overhead arm position opens up the chest cavity and straightens the spine. It begins and ends with mountain pose.

Shoulder stand

1 You lie flat on your back and slowly raise your extended legs into a vertical position.

2 Next raise your pelvis off the floor and brace your hips with your hands.

3 Now slowly and carefully lower your legs over your head to the floor.

4 In the final phase you bend your knees.

5 Now slowly roll back into starting position.

Did this peak your curiosity? If we kindled your interest, find out more about the correct execution of poses in special yoga books and in yoga classes.

Training Shooting Sports

Progressive muscle relaxation

When you are restless, anxious and unfocused, it isn't always easy to calm yourself. This trick helps: first tense up, then relax! Consciously tense up certain muscles or parts of your body and after briefly holding, you relax almost automatically. This is called progressive muscle relaxation.

To do these exercises, get into a comfortable position, either lying down or seated.

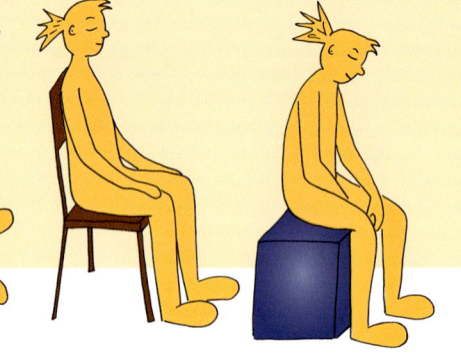

This is how you practice:

- Tense the respective muscles.
- As you do so, breathe normally.
- You feel the tension without cramping or experiencing pain.
- Hold the tension for about 5-10 seconds.
- Release the tension and rest for about 30 seconds.
- Now you can feel the complete loosening of the muscles and sense the relaxation.

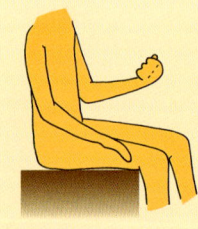

Hand and forearm

Slowly make a tight fist and feel the tension in your hand and forearm. After 5-10 seconds, release the tension. Switch hands.

Biceps

Bend your elbows bringing your hands to your shoulders. This tightens the muscles on the front of the upper arm (biceps). Try to keep your hands relaxed.

It's All in the Mind

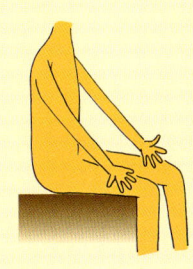

Triceps

Turn your palms face up and extend your arms. Press your palms against your legs or a table. Now you can feel the tension in the back of the upper arm (triceps).

Shoulders

Pull your shoulders up to your ears. Feel the tension in the shoulders.

Face

Now "scrunch up" your face! Clench your teeth, squeeze your eyes shut and tighten the muscles into a scary grimace.

Back

Tighten your back muscles by pulling your shoulder blades together.

Stomach

You can tighten the stomach by sucking it in or pushing it out.

Thighs and buttocks

Squeeze your butt and tighten your thigh muscles.

Lower legs

Sit in a relaxed position and pull your toes up towards your face. At the same time the muscles along the shin and the calves try to "tight" against this movement.

Did this peak your curiosity? If we kindled your interest, find out more about the correct execution of these exercises in special books on progressive relaxation or in classes.

Training Shooting Sports

Relaxation

Anxiety, pressure, distraction, tension, – none of these things are great for a stable firing position.

On the previous pages we gave a brief introduction to **yoga** and **progressive muscle relaxation**. Of course there are many other ways to attune to the impending task. Try whatever feels good to you and what you can manage. Ask your trainer and experienced athletes or check out one of the many reference books.

Teaching yourself

With this method of self-relaxation you give yourself instructions for relaxation. You can influence the individual parts of your body with formulaic phrases like: "My leg is getting really heavy!" or "My stomach is getting soft and warm!"

Exercise

Taking a walk, jogging, cycling or swimming clear the head and loosen the muscles. Think about happy experiences or other pleasant things to put yourself in a positive frame of mind for the competition.

Music and conversation

Pleasant, soothing music is relaxing. With headphones you can easily shield yourself from the outside world and "submerge" yourself in your own world. Pleasant conversation (no discussions or verbal disputes) with friends gives you the necessary composure.

But a certain amount of anxiety is necessary for a successful competition result. Don't overdo the relaxation because a "sleeping pill" doesn't have the necessary bite!

It's All in the Mind

Self-confidence

Some say, "Self-confidence is half the battle!" Of course it isn't quite that simple, but there is some truth to that saying. Someone, whose approach is self-confident, who believes in himself and his ability certainly has a better chance at success than someone who is afraid and full of doubt. But you shouldn't get reckless and make mistakes because of too much confidence!

> He, he! You guys are no match for me! You don't stand a chance against my willpower! What are you clowns even doing here?

> Oh Boy! It's not going to work out again! I'm just plain bad and always get a low ring score. When I see the others I just want to go home.

Which of the following qualities and attitudes can you as a shooting athlete benefit from, and which are more of a hindrance? Cross out anything you don't want to have too much of.

Self-confidence – enjoy training – self-doubt – blind rage – willingness to take risks – impatience – being laid-back – fear of making mistakes – ambition – desire to win – faith in one's performance – fear of failure – bad mood – feeling in great form – attentiveness – concentration – cockiness.

Training Shooting Sports

Even the best athlete loses sometimes

When you are not focused enough sometimes, don't have enough strength, the strikes don't hit the expected mark or your ranking is much too low, you will ask yourself where the problem lies. Maybe you weren't in good form, the shooting range wasn't right for you or the opponents were better than you. They have trained longer and therefore are stronger. Don't be angry, but keep on practicing, make a detailed analysis and together with the trainer decide on measures for your continued training.

Record these measures, goals and results in a training diary!

It's All in the Mind

But if you think you should have done better, then think about the reasons and causes. A chart on which you can list reasons for your poor performance and training measures can help you with that.

What was I dissatisfied with?	What were the reasons?	What do I want to do in the near future?
Bad start at the competition	Too few practice shots	Starting phase training
Bad shots	Trigger pull errors	Trigger pull training
Unstable firing position	Zero point was not ok	Setting up and zero point check

Training Shooting Sports

Test

How would you react in the following situations?

1. **Situation:** You don't feel like going to practice.

   A Of course you stay home because you shouldn't force yourself to do anything. — 1
   B You go to practice without much enthusiasm because you don't want to disappoint your parents. — 2
   C You go to practice like always because if you miss you'll get worse again. Maybe you'll feel like practicing once you're at the shooting range. — 3

2. **Situation:** The trainer repeatedly criticizes you for having your trigger finger on the side of the grip.

   A It is aggravating that I'm still doing it the wrong way. But I'm just glad the shot lands on the target. — 2
   B He shouldn't always be so petty. It's not a beauty contest. One more word and I'm gone! — 1
   C It's good that the trainer is always watching. Then little mistakes like this can't even sneak in. — 3

3. **Situation:** The opponent is particularly strong at the start.

   A You breathe calmly, check your firing position and concentrate on your sights. — 3
   B You think, I have no influence over what the opponent does, so I better just concentrate on myself! — 2
   C You're afraid you'll "mess up" the shot. After all, the opponent is bound to make you nervous and you'll get a bad score. — 1

It's All in the Mind

4. Situation: Last week the trainer said that Tom will be in the team lineup instead of you.

A You think that's tough luck but you probably weren't good enough. — 2
B You're sore because you're at least as good as Tom. Hopefully he won't do well and then you can say: "I would have been better!" — 1
C You help Tom and support him in whatever he needs. You work hard at practice so next time you will be in the lineup again. — 3

5. Situation: The shot was totally off the mark.

A No wonder! I was blinded by the light and couldn't see a thing! — 1
B That is aggravating but now I'll concentrate on the next shot. — 3
C The competition is almost over and my concentration is starting to fade. — 2

6. Situation: The shooter in the neighboring stand always puts down his firearm with the chamber closed.

A You immediately confront the shooter and remind him of the important safety rules at the shooting range. — 3
B You go to see the trainer and tell him what the other shooter is doing wrong. — 2
C You think to yourself: "That's not my problem!" and keep on practicing. — 1

Add up your points! You will find the score in the solutions section.

Training Shooting Sports

"Brain training"
Test your imagination

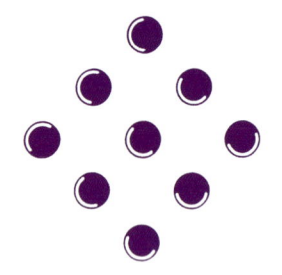

1 Connections

Connect these nine dots in one stroke with straight, contiguous lines!

2 Matches

By moving three matches you will end up with three equal size squares. Try it!

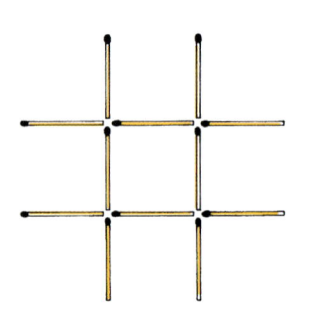

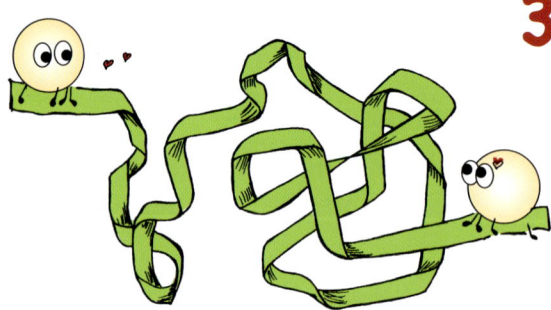

3 Ribbon walk

Once upon a time there was a bug in love, who walked on a ribbon to get to his true love. Will he make it or will he end up on the back of the ribbon?

4 Triangles

Look closely at the adjacent drawing. How many triangles do you see?

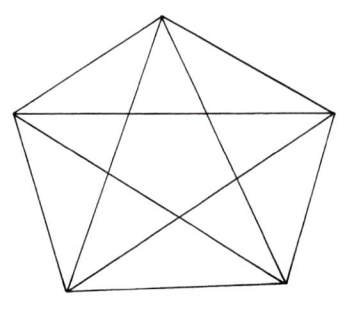

7 Technique

Whenever we learn something new, we must familiarize ourselves with the appropriate, necessary techniques. First you learn the basics, then you build on them and continue to prefect them through lots of practice. There will be setbacks and mistakes, but you will learn from them!

That is how you learned to walk, write, swim and ride a bike, etc. The motion sequence was explained, demonstrated, and you were encouraged to practice on your own.

Anyone who wants to be successful as a shooting athlete must immerse himself in the technique of shooting sports. This includes the correct firing position in the various positions, aiming, firing, follow-through and breathing. There are many details you must pay attention to.

A good shooting athlete takes many years to master the techniques. They are continuously improved upon and modified. That definitely comes with regular training and through competing

During ongoing training new techniques continue to be added and familiar techniques are perfected.

Training Shooting Sports

Movements are automated

When you are at the shooting stand, you have to concentrate on your tasks, control your breathing and plan the process. You do not have time to think about your arm or leg position.

The techniques must be practiced until they work perfectly every time. In training you will practice the techniques and motion sequences again and again until you no longer have to think about every single step. Then you will know the placement of your feet and the position of your arms by heart.

*How did that go again?
Which leg is in the front?
And then the right shoulder,
or was it the elbow?
What do I do with the feet?*

What kind of nonsense is this? Why don't you just get in position?

Oh coach, I can't remember how I'm supposed to stand!

Technique

Technique training

Whenever you learn a new technique, the trainer usually introduces it with an explanation and a demonstration. He outlines the motion sequence, tells you what you have to pay particular attention to and which mistakes to avoid.

As in school, there are different learning methods for learning shooting sports. Just as people are different, they also have different ways of learning something new. The trainer will discuss the different learning types and introduce the new material through different methods. What is successful often is a blend of various learning methods.

In order for learning to be successful, you must have an interest in learning and the desire to learn!

Ways of learning

- ☐ The trainer explains the new technique.
- ☐ The trainer or another player demonstrates the technique.
- ☐ The new technique is shown via drawings or sequence pictures.
- ☐ Possible mistakes are discussed with the aid of error images.
- ☐ Videos are shown.
- ☐ The trainer asks the athletes to describe and explain the new technique.
- ☐ The athletes make sketches.
- ☐ They try the new technique themselves.
- ☐ The technique is executed with monitoring and suggestions by the trainer.
- ☐ The technique is executed with monitoring and suggestions by training buddies.
- ☐ The athletes do dry exercises without firearms.

What learning type are you? Check the learning methods that are most helpful to you when learning a new technique. Try out what works best for you!

Training Shooting Sports

Perseverance brings success

Of course you're curious and it is lots of fun to learn and try out a new technique. In the beginning the movements tend to be fairly vague, you watch the angle of your feet and make sure that your arms and legs are doing everything right. You quickly see some progress. Your movements become surer and faster.

But gradually all that practicing gets dull. You no longer notice an obvious improvement in your performance and the thrill of something new is gone as well. You think that things are already going pretty well with this new technique. Why keep practicing? Now comes the point when you may not feel like doing it anymore. The key now is "perseverance", or you will forget some things and all that previous practicing was for nothing. So remember what you have resolved to do and fight your "inner couch potato"!

Technique

The road to increased performance

After that quick progress there will be many training days when you will feel like nothing is happening. It is important to know that this stage will come. On the long road to perfect technique there are always stages of quick progress, and also stages of grinding drudgery. So if you think it can't get any better and you have already reached your performance capacity and any more practice is useless, keep on trying and you will see that it does get better.

During this apparent standstill your body is preparing for the next level of performance development. You could say it is getting internally reprogrammed for the next step. So don't let an apparent standstill drive you to despair. These are necessary transitional phases. The key is: Perseverance!

Some techniques you will learn relatively quickly. Others require many, many hours of training, even years. Rest assured—persistent and arduous training pays off!

Tips for technique training

- Listen and watch closely when the technique is being explained, shown through pictures, and demonstrated.
- Mentally retrace the technique, and with your eyes closed concentrate on visualizing the sequence and the movement.
- At practice, try the technique over and over again in different situations. Monitor yourself after every repetition or have others observe what needs improvement.
- Take your time looking over the illustrations and going through the descriptions and comparing them to your movements.
- It helps to explain, describe and show the technique to someone else. Monitor and help each other!

In the end, the technique should be executed quickly, accurately and almost automatically. The progressions are "programmed" and stored in your brain through the many repetitions.

Training Shooting Sports

If you don't work hard at practice, are unfocused and sloppy, the wrong sequences will be stored. When something incorrect has been automated, it will take a lot of effort to break that habit again later. Unlearning is more difficult than learning!

Monitoring – Evaluating – improving

Don't learn anything that is incorrect and automate it! That is why you need to monitor the progression of a new technique, recognize the mistakes and execute the movement with more and more accuracy. How quickly that works also depends on your goals and your motivation.

I don't get it! Only a month ago, you praised me for my stance, and today I did it exactly the same and I'm being criticized!

But that's normal! A month ago, you had practiced for the first time, and that was great! But now you have to keep getting better!

You reach many sub-goals on the road to perfect technique, and every little mistake is observed and corrected. Evaluation by the trainer is best since he knows the most about shooting sports.

Technique

Muscle sense

People often talk about the five senses you should use when you want to learn something new. What that means is that you should listen well, watch carefully, touch it, smell it and taste it. Surely you have noticed that not all senses are always used simultaneously and equally as much.

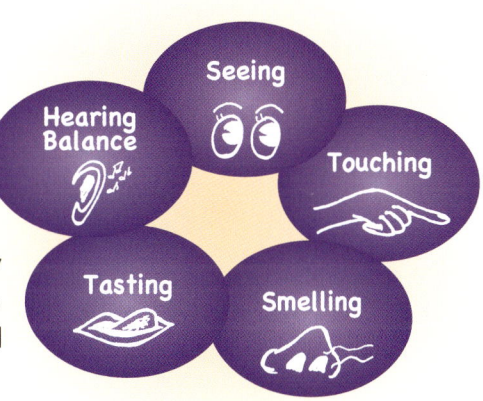

Senses that are important in shooting sports

You certainly can't taste anything when you are shooting. Smelling is more of a secondary effect when the shooting range smells like oil or spent ammunition, or when there are many athletes at the range. That you need to see to shoot doesn't require an explanation. But during a competition you also have to be able to hear: the shot rhythm and the bullet entry. Part of the sensory organ called the ear is also your sense of balance. You need that to keep your equilibrium.

Some people even talk about a sixth sense. Shooting athletes need such a sixth sense for the muscle sense or sense of movement. We will simply call it **muscle sense**. It is very important for learning and mastering technique in shooting sports. At the shooting range you get set up, take aim at the target and control your breathing. You must have "a feel" for the correct foot position, how high you hold your arms, and your head position. You can feel the position of your body without looking. Add to that index finger sensitivity for the pre-draw and trigger pull.

This "feel" is only acquired by practicing diligently in training.

85

Training Shooting Sports

Sensitization program

Preliminary exercises

- *Firing position drill without a firearm.*
- *Firing position drill at actual target height.*

Dry run

- *Practicing an actual sequence with a firearm and dry-fire at actual target height.*

Combination training at the stand

- *One dry-shot (preparation for "ideal" shot).*
- *One live shot (actual shot).*
- *One mental shot (evaluation of "ideal" shot).*

Balance exercises

- *Dry run and live run on various floor surfaces, air cushions, mats, etc.*

Technique

Practice with disruption

"Everybody be quiet, – I have to concentrate!" Well, that probably only works at practice. At a competition no one will be that considerate. A door bangs shut, something drops on the floor or the neighboring shooter talks to himself. How are you supposed to concentrate with all that? It can be done if you consciously train with these disruptions. You also allow disruptions during training and even incorporate them intentionally!

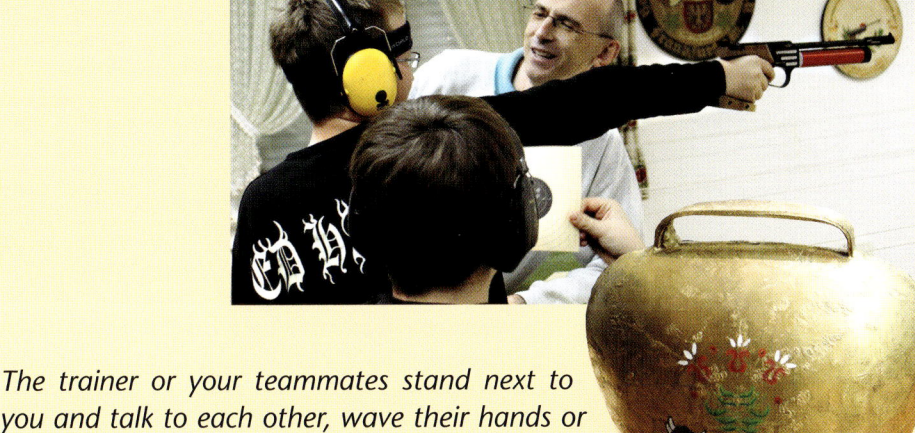

The trainer or your teammates stand next to you and talk to each other, wave their hands or make sudden loud noises. But you try to not let it affect you!

We know of a club that owns a famous cowbell. It can clang so loud that the shooter has to really utilize all of his concentration techniques.

You will continue to handle disruptions with more and more confidence and will be less and less affected by them!

Training Shooting Sports

Have you had a laugh today?

"Our trainer has a terrible memory!"
"Does he forget everything?"
"On the contrary, he doesn't forget anything!"

Says Tom to Tina: "You are wearing one blue and one yellow shoe!"
"Yes, isn't it strange? And I have another pair just like this one at home!"

The trainer is disappointed: "Your shooting score today leaves much to be desired!" Answers Tina: "Well, then I desire a large scoop of ice cream!"

"What would you do if you shot as many rings as I do?"
"Definitely practice a lot more!"

Two frogs sit at the edge of a pond. One frog says: "Ribbit!" Answers the other one: "I was just about to say that!"

........8 Rifle Shooting

Since the invention of gunpowder, rifle shooting has been one of the oldest types of shooting. However, today's hi-tech sports equipment barely resembles the initial muzzleloader models. The majority of shooting athletes find rifle shooting fascinating.

The Olympic rifle disciplines include:

	Men	Women
Air rifle	60 shots	40 shots
3-position small bore	3x40 free rifle	3x20 sports rifle
Small bore prone	60 shots	-

You can find a list of events for all age groups, regional and national competitions as well as regulations on the National Rifle Association's website. International competitions are conducted according to the ISSF (the international umbrella organization).

Training Shooting Sports

Standing firing position

The standing firing position posture is actually a very shaky structure because the narrow upright body is supported by a rather small base. This automatically leads to some swaying. The standing firing position therefore requires a precise working sense of position and placement and a good sense of balance.

Firing position procedure

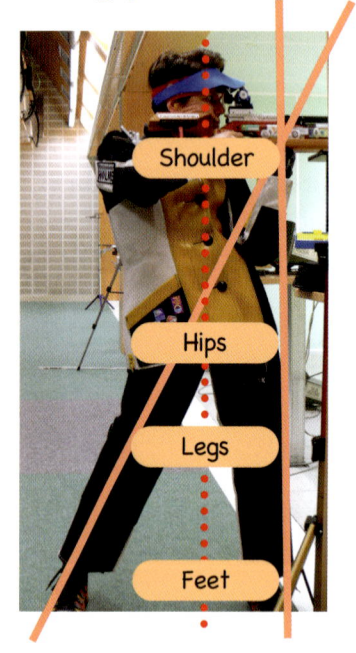

The standing firing position is constructed from the bottom up. The feet are placed parallel to each other and form the base. Next the appropriate leg, hip, shoulder, arm and head positions are defined. The firing position is established through good relative placement and coordinated muscle activity.

To better balance the weight of the firearm, your center of gravity lies in the front third of the distance between your feet.

Holding the firearm in the correct position requires, among other things, the four contact points that are needed to establish a clean zero point on the target.

1 Insertion point of the butt plate at the shoulder.
2 Position of supporting hand underneath the front shaft.
3 Position of the trigger hand on the pistol grip, including trigger finger on the trigger.
4 Position of the head on the stock.

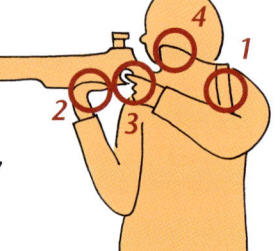

Rifle Shooting

Foot position

The feet form the "base" of your firing position.

The lines of the feet are parallel to each other and at a 90° angle to the bore sight.

For good balance the contact of the soles of your feet with the floor must be evenly distributed.

Your toes play an important part in your ability to balance. To be fully effective they must have sufficient room inside the shooting shoes.

The feet are shoulder-width or slightly farther, apart.

1 Smaller shooting athletes often prefer a wider stance.
2 The rear leg can be set back slightly to support the firing position to the back and to keep the hip from rotating inward.
3 Turning your toes slightly inward gives you a more stable stance.
4 The right foot (for right-handed shooters) determines, among other things, the height of the zero point:
   • Narrower stance – zero point goes down.
   • Wider stance – zero point goes up.

Leg position

The legs are straight but the knees are not locked. The forward leg is slightly more vertical than the rear leg.

Hip position

The hip is positioned parallel to the line of fire and pushed forward in direction of the target. This creates a vertical column on which the supporting arm and the firearm can be easily positioned.

Upper body

Your upper body leans back slightly and your relaxed breathing allows you to "sink" into a deep stance. All of the participating vertebrae and bones form a stable unit.

Training Shooting Sports

When in firing position, make sure your legs are relatively relaxed without compromising your fixed hip position!

Shoulder position

The right shoulder is relaxed and passively holds the butt plate in the right position.

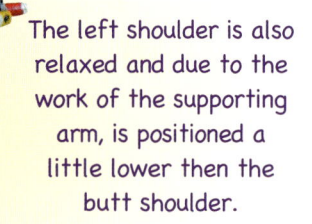

The left shoulder is also relaxed and due to the work of the supporting arm, is positioned a little lower then the butt shoulder.

Supporting arm

- The weight of the rifle rests on the supporting arm.
- The elbow should ideally rest on the hip or pelvic bone.
- As seen from the front, firearm, elbow, hip, knee and foot form a vertical line.
- To create an advantageous angle from upper to lower arm you should not grip too close to the trigger, but also not too far forward on the front shaft. The firearm must be balanced.

If the bulk of the firearm's weight is in front of the supporting hand, it can cause cramping and shaking. That will have a negative effect on the shot.

Supporting hand

You can rest the firearm underneath the forward shaft on your palm, in the cradle between thumb and index finger, or on a balled fist. In the field you will see many variations. What's important is that you find a hand position that allows you to establish a sight picture at a level with the bull's eye. Positions with a straight wrist work well.

Get a well-fitting shooting glove to help support your wrist and fingers while bracing!

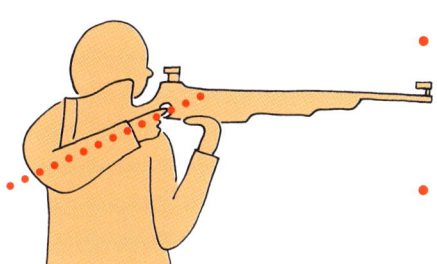

Rifle Shooting

Trigger hand

- The trigger hand firmly grips the pistol grip so that the three points – supporting hand, shoulder and trigger hand- form a solid link.
- The trigger arm as an extension of the straight wrist slopes down towards the elbow, but only as far as the contact between stock and shoulder remains intact.

Firearm position

Place the rifle into the shoulder pocket with the butt plate and firm your grip on the pistol grip until you feel the rifle firmly anchored at the shoulder. The necessary pressure between shoulder and stock will result from the correct stock length and the correct position of the butt plate.

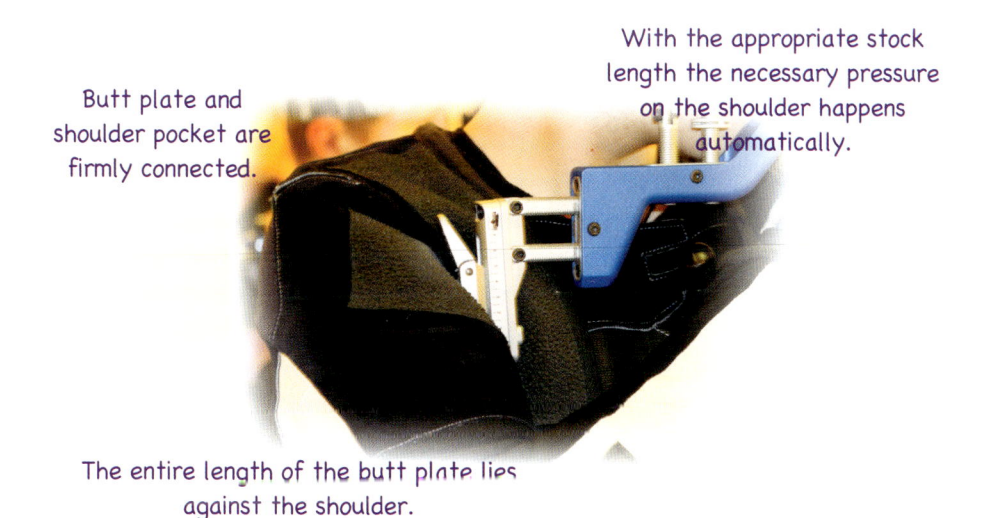

Butt plate and shoulder pocket are firmly connected.

With the appropriate stock length the necessary pressure on the shoulder happens automatically.

The entire length of the butt plate lies against the shoulder.

If the butt plate keeps sliding off your shoulder, your elbow is either too low or you are not pressing the butt plate firmly enough into the shoulder, but rather on the upper arm!

Training Shooting Sports

Head position

The shooting athlete's fourth contact point with the firearm is the head. The position of the head is crucial to the overall balance. Of course an erect head position works best.

The rifle is slightly canted toward the head.

You rest only the weight of your head on the stock.

Your eye looks through the middle of the diopter.

The muscles of your neck and the back of your neck are relatively relaxed.

- The head doesn't go to the rifle, but the rifle comes to the head!
- You adjust the comb so that ear, eye and sights are on one sight line. Then your vision will be centered.

Zero point

- You position the axis of your hips parallel to the shooting axis, vertically to the bulls' eye.
- After placing your feet and placing the firearm, you make a minor adjustment to your position.
- You correct with a minimal rotation of the entire system.
- Now you place your cheek back against the comb with your eyes closed and check your sight picture. If you can see the bull's eye centered through all sights, you have reached the zero point.

Rifle Shooting

Every little change to the foot position or hip position changes your sight picture. Make sure you have a "clean" zero point when you set up your firing position!

Internal firing position

Surely you have heard the term internal firing position at practice or from grown-ups. It refers to the tensing of muscles in the entire body. Some muscles are completely relaxed while others are working really hard. In firing position and while taking the shot, the perfect muscle tension is always the same, regardless of whether you are in perfect shape, highly focused, nervous or already a little lackadaisical.

Once you have placed the rifle against the shoulder, close your eyes and take deliberate breaths. That's the best way to turn your focus to the inside.

The head is lowered to the stock.

The shoulders are relaxed.

Back muscles are tightened.

The legs are relaxed.

The trigger hand grips tightly.

The trigger arm is relaxed.

The trigger finger is relaxed and limber.

The supporting arm bears the weight of the firearm.

The feet bear the body weight. It is distributed between toes and heels.

While in firing position, take a "journey trough the body" and take note of what feels right and what doesn't from the bottom up. Talk to your trainer about it!

95

Training Shooting Sports

Prone firing position

The prone firing position is first in the 3-position competition as well as a separate discipline in the individual and team events. In the prone position it is possible to score higher ring numbers because:

- Due to the large support surface, the firing position is very stable.
- The body's center of gravity is very low.
- You can be more relaxed in this firing position because the weight of the firearm is partially born by the shooting sling.

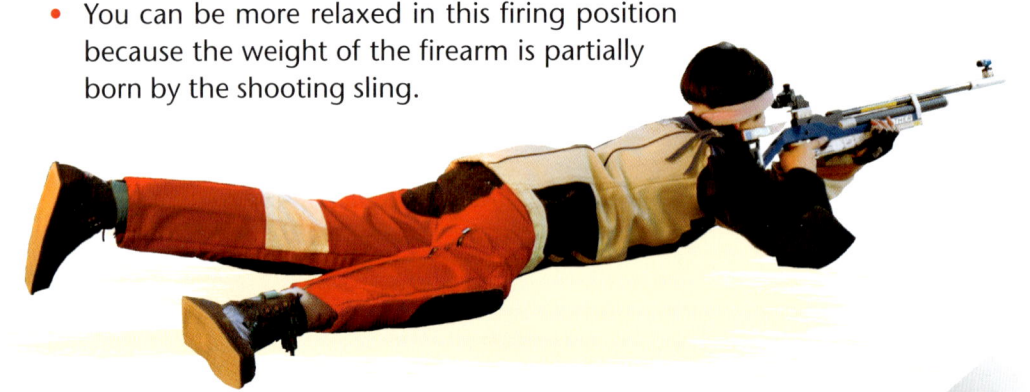

To be successful your body must be relaxed! Trying to imitate technical images will just make you tense up. Use our advice as a guideline and find your own position!

Body

The body should be positioned at a 0° to 30° angle to the shooting direction. The shoulder joint should ideally be parallel to the target. The placement of the right arm changes the position of the shoulder joint.

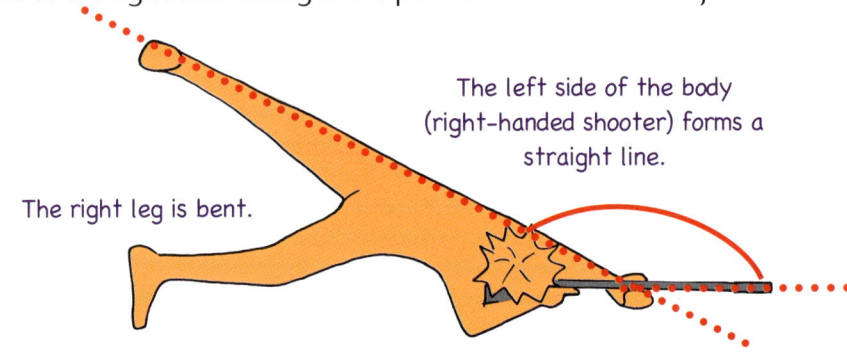

The left side of the body (right-handed shooter) forms a straight line.

The right leg is bent.

Rifle Shooting

Legs

In the prone firing position you have two options for the placement of your right leg (right-handed shooter):

- An **extended leg** provides a lower body position.
- A **bent leg** reinforces the contact between shoulder and firearm.

Supporting hand

- Your left hand should be placed on the underside of the stock so it lies across the ball of your thumb.
- To prevent tensing and instability, the stock should not lie too far into the palm.
- You fingers are relaxed and open.

Handstop

- Your hand is on the hand stop right between the thumb and index finger.
- The shooting sling runs across the back of your hand.
- Your hand position on the stock depends on the length of your arm.

You can increase the pressure of the butt plate against your shoulder by sliding the hand stop forward on the forearm, fastening the sling higher up on the arm or shortening it. But be careful: If the hand stop is too far forward, it can cause lateral misses and the correct shoulder position is lost, respectively.

Training Shooting Sports

Positioning the firearm

The firearm should be placed as far as possible to the inside, near the neck, next to the collarbone. This allows you to keep your head relatively straight, recoil will strike more toward the middle of the body and a lateral deflection of the firearm during the shot can be reduced.

The entire length of the butt plate must lie firmly against the shoulder. Pressure against the shoulder should be at least equal to the pressure on the hand stop.

Trigger arm

The trigger arm serves as a brace and must ensure a technically flawless shot.

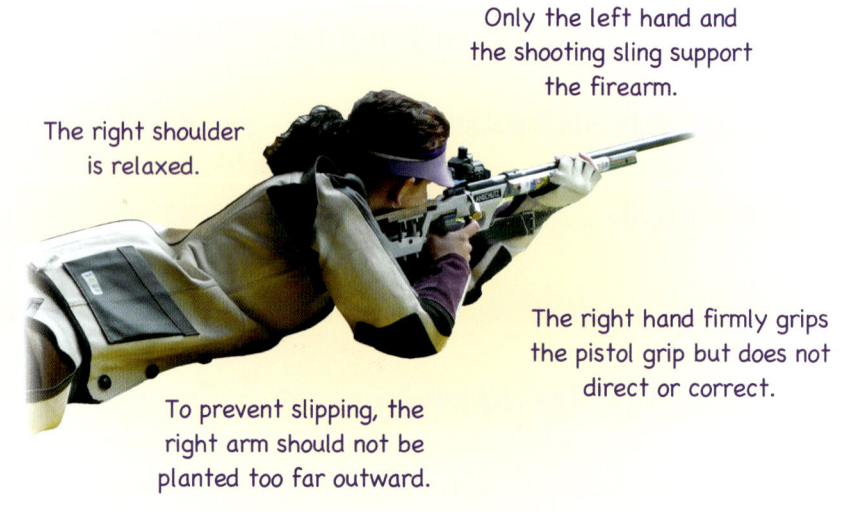

Only the left hand and the shooting sling support the firearm.

The right shoulder is relaxed.

The right hand firmly grips the pistol grip but does not direct or correct.

To prevent slipping, the right arm should not be planted too far outward.

Check your firing position by slightly loosening your right hand from the grip. Does the firearm still point at the bull's eye?

Rifle Shooting

Head position

Due to the special head position the cheek puts a certain amount of pressure on the comb and thereby on the firearm. It is therefore particularly important to apply consistent pressure when taking a shot.

For perfect and consistent cheek pressure, the comb must be accurately adjusted for the shooter.

Zero point

Once the firing position is established and after the subsequent total relaxation of the arms and the right shoulder, the firearm must point directly at the bull's eye.

Set-up sequence

1. *By positioning the trigger arm on the pad the body-firearm system is grounded.*
2. *You get into firing position with your eyes closed and relax your muscles.*
3. *You open your eyes and check the deviation from the bull's eye.*

Correcting lateral deviation

- In case of *minor deviation*, leave the support elbow in place and reposition the trigger elbow as needed.
- In case of *major deviation*, abandon the firing position and correct the angle of your body position.

Correcting vertical deviation

- Shifting the upper body.
- Adjusting the butt plate.
- Adjusting the length of the shooting sling.
- Moving the hand stop.

Training Shooting Sports

Kneeling firing position

In rifle shooting this discipline is quite difficult and usually will be learned much later. The shooter must have perfect balance and a good breathing technique.

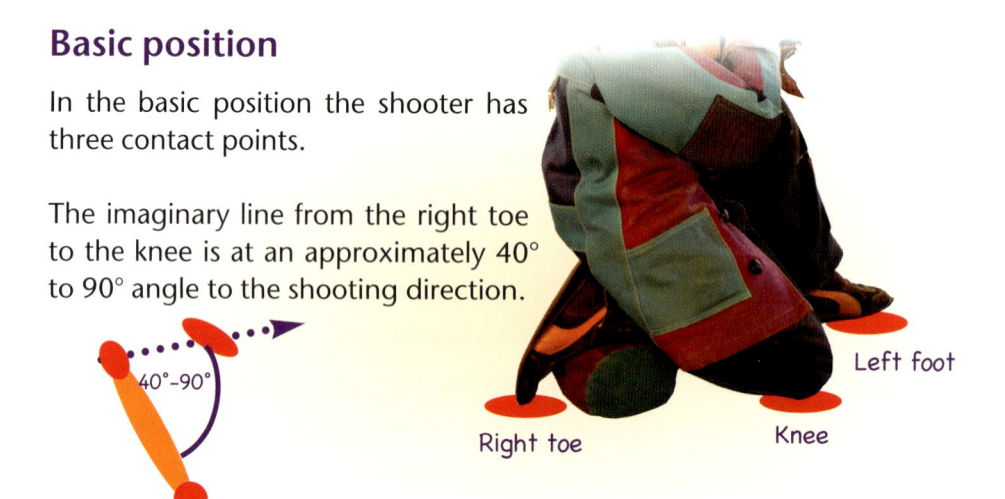

Basic position

In the basic position the shooter has three contact points.

The imaginary line from the right toe to the knee is at an approximately 40° to 90° angle to the shooting direction.

Position on the kneeling roll

A stable position of the right leg and foot is particularly important for a successful kneeling firing position.

- Set down the top of your right foot at a right angle to the kneeling roll so the toe and knee are firmly planted on the pad.

- Adjust the roll so there is more weight on the foot than the knee.
- The toe of the right foot points to the back.
- Now you can sit on your heel with the middle of your backside.

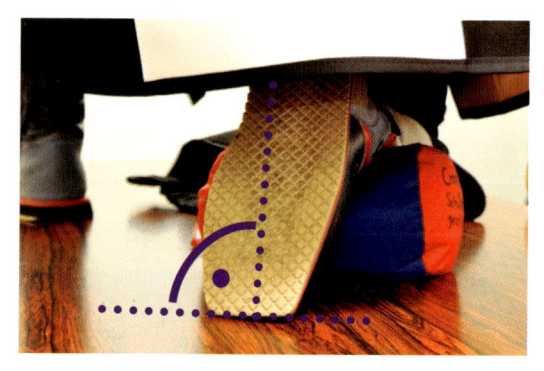

Rifle Shooting

The kneeling roll makes the kneeling firing position more stable and comfortable. The kneeling roll is a cylindrical cushion, no more than 9.84 inches long, has a diameter of no more than 7.6 inches, and is filled with PVC pellets, rice, grains or grass seed. Tying it off with laces or straps is not permitted.

Since the stability of the entire firing position depends on the firm position of the toe, you should wear a special shooting shoe with a rigid sole.

Supporting leg

The supporting leg provides the substructure for the supporting arm and thereby is responsible for the overall stability. It must bear and balance the weight of the upper body and the rifle and can not tense up while doing so. You have to determine the most favorable position for the supporting leg yourself by experimenting and making minute corrections.

Effects of various leg positions

- **Slightly forward (far forward for shooters with long legs) position of the supporting leg in shooting direction:** *(see photo)*

    The pressure on the lower leg slants forward, which makes it easier to balance the weight of the firearm and the upper body. *(Recommended!)*

- **Vertical position of the lower leg, or even slightly behind the vertical line:**
    The firing position tends to tilt forward.

- **Rotating the foot to the inside:**
    Increases lateral stability of the lower leg.

101

Training Shooting Sports

Upper body

In **upright kneeling position** the upper body is nearly vertical. The bulk of the weight is on the right leg, the heel and the kneeling roll. The advantages of this position are that your head is loose, your shoulders are relaxed and the supporting arm and supporting leg are unladen. The disadvantages are the high center of gravity and the minimal resistance to recoil.

In the **forward kneeling position** the upper body leans forward and the bulk of the weight is thus shifted to the supporting leg. A well-chosen position is particularly important here to avoid a tensing of the muscles in the supporting leg.

The center of gravity should be between the supporting foot and the kneeling roll.

Supporting arm

To be able to properly support the rifle the supporting arm is deliberately positioned on the knee of the supporting leg. There are various options for this. Figure out which one works best for you!

- Set the elbow in the indentation between kneecap and thigh that forms when the knee is bent.
- The indentation between elbow and upper arm that forms when the arm is bent rests on the kneecap.
- Position the point of the elbow in front of the knee.
- Position the point of the elbow behind the knee.

As per regulations, the point of the elbow must not be more than 3.9 inches over or 5.8 inches behind the point of the knee.

Fastening the shooting sling

The shooting sling unburdens the supporting arm and thereby stabilizes the firing position. You can fasten the shooting sling at the upper arm closer to the underarm or closer to the elbow joint. This keeps the pulse from being transferred to the firearm. Should you however fasten the sling in the middle of the elbow you must pull it tight enough so it doesn't slip. But be careful not to obstruct your blood circulation.

Tips on how to position the firearm, the head, and how to fire can be found in the section on the prone firing position!

Pulse

In the kneeling firing position, the pulse can be a problem because the rhythmic beat can affect the firearm. An intensified pulse is often caused by wrinkles in the jacket, tight pants or a badly adjusted shooting sling. Make sure you have sufficient freedom of movement and check your clothing!

Zero point

In case of **lateral deviation** from the bull's eye you must adjust your basic position accordingly. In doing so, you maintain all of the existing angles – you move your body as if it were on a turntable.

If the deviation is too great, you should get up and rotate the kneeling roll to redo your set-up!

Vertical deviations up or down can be corrected as follows:

- Adjust the butt plate, move the hand stop **and** shooting sling. (The firing position pressure ratios must be accurate!)
- Slight shift forward or back of the supporting leg.
- Major corrections can be made with more or less fill in the kneeling roll.

Training Shooting Sports

Taking aim

When you take aim you point the firearm at the bull's eye. In doing so you line up the eye, diopter, front sight and the bull's eye.

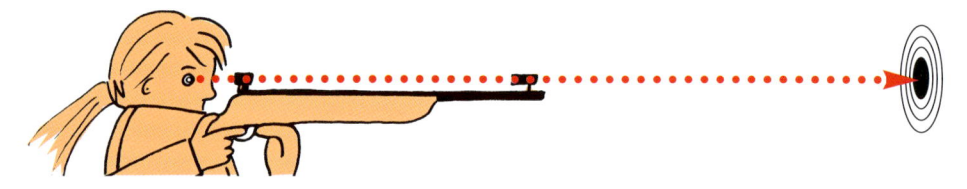

Aiming technique

- When taking perfect aim you look through the exact center of the diopter and the front sight tunnel.
- Next the bull's eye is centered in the aperture.
- Now the sight picture appears as one unit.
- An even convergence is apparent in a tight shot group.

Target time

You should not exceed a target time of **eight seconds** because your eye is not able to focus on the sight picture indefinitely. The result will be inaccurate.

If the target time takes too long, stop and start over!

Rifle Shooting

The eye

If the external firing position is accurate, your body is relaxed, the cheek lies against the comb and everything is focused on the target, the eye takes over the additional aiming process. Your eyes see the sights approaching the bull's eye. Now the rifle position can still be adjusted.

Try to avoid alternating between light (sun, lamp) and dark (bull's eye) because it always takes a while for the pupil to dilate. (Also see chapter 9, "pistol shooting".)

Diopter

The diopter allows you to accurately align the point of impact. You can change the point of impact by turning (clicking) the set screws. The iris is attached to the diopter. The iris disc can have a diameter of 0.5 – 3.0 mm and should be adjusted so the front sight is clearly visible. But this also depends on the distance between your eye and the iris. The ideal distance is between 1.57 and 2.75 inches.

Front sight

Since every eye sees the distance between the bull's eye and the edge of the front sight differently, it is not possible to recommend an ideal aperture size. The basic rule of thumb is: the greater the sight picture deviations in firing position, the greater the distance between the bull's eye and the front sight should be (about a third of the bull's eye diameter.)

Let your trainer advise you on the choice and setting of a diopter and front sight. He will match the equipment to your firing position and level of expertise.

105

Sight line elevation

Sight line elevation is a blessing for anyone with a particularly long neck and/or sloping shoulders. It is a way to raise the diopter and front sight tunnel on the barrel.

Advantage: Less tension in the back of the neck, the head is more erect, shorter distance to lower the head to the comb.

Disadvantage: Only suitable for advanced shooters who are able to tilt the firearm evenly.

Pulling the trigger

A clean trigger pull means the shot is released without transferring the motion to the firearm.

Trigger hand

Your wrist is as straight as possible.

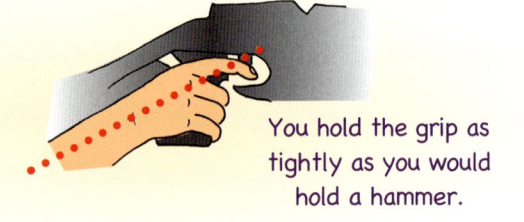

You hold the grip as tightly as you would hold a hammer.

Trigger finger

The trigger finger motion is straight back and parallel to the barrel. The trigger is released with the first phalanx of the trigger finger because the middle of the first phalanx (pad) is most sensitive. This ensures rectilinearity and prevents lateral force.

- When you have reached the pressure point, the trigger finger position is at approximately 90° to the shooting direction.
- Make sure only the trigger finger moves when you pull the trigger and that its movement does not transfer to other fingers, the hand or the firearm.
- The trigger finger always lies in the same spot on the lever. It does not touch anything else and is able to move freely.

Rifle Shooting

Trigger techniques

Choose one of the four trigger techniques based on your personal skill level.

1. **Subconscious trigger pull:**
   Pressure increases evenly until the shot breaks. (Often used in prone position and by beginners).

2. **Progressive trigger pull:**
   The pressure rhythmically increases or decreases incrementally until the shot breaks. (Somewhat problematic, too risky for the beginner because the shot can break unexpectedly!)

3. **Dynamic trigger pull:**
   This type of trigger pull is also referred to as "yanking" the trigger. (Not suitable for beginners because the shot easily misses.)

4. **Conscious trigger pull:**
   The pressure rapidly increases to a point just short of the full trigger pull weight. Depending on the situation, the final phase concludes quickly or softly. (It is often used by top athletes, or those who aspire to be …!)

Trigger characteristics

Triggers can be adjusted differently. We generally differentiate between two types:

Trigger with pre-pull
As with the air rifle, you first move past the pre-pull weight to get to the pressure point. Now you must increase the pressure to release the shot. You aremore likely to fire a controlled shot with this type oftrigger.

Direct trigger
This type of trigger has only one phase. There is no pre-pull. The trigger travels past the entire trigger pull weight at only one point in the trigger travel. This trigger is only suitable for experts because it requires a very sensitive touch.

Training Shooting Sports

Trigger pull force / trigger pull weight

This refers to the amount of force the athlete must apply to push past the pressure on the trigger in order to release a shot. The lower the resistance setting the more easily the shot will break. In the beginning you start out with a higher trigger pull weight setting because the trigger finger sensitivity has yet to be developed.

Ask your trainer about your trigger pull weight and ask him to show you how to adjust the trigger.

Trigger pull mistakes

The most common mistakes:
- Yanking due to nervousness or low temperatures.
- Uneven pressure increase – playing with the pressure.
- Trigger pull drags because fingers make contact with the firearm.
- Finger does not always have the same point of contact with the lever.
- Diagonal pull because the trigger hand is positioned incorrectly on the grip.
- Trigger finger is held against the side of the lever.

Follow-through

The follow-through is an important technical element that immediately follows the release of the shot. After the shot breaks you must remain in firing position for one to two seconds to "follow" the shot.

Reasons for the follow-through are:
- The shot ends smoothly.
- Dismantling the firing position too soon can have a negative effect on the firing.
- During the follow-through you can already check and analyze deviation, firing position and reaction as the shot breaks.
- By watching the muzzle as the shot is released, you can already make decisions on necessary corrective measures, e.g. diopter setting or external firing position.

Rifle Shooting

Breathing

Breathing supplies your body with vital oxygen, lets you control your anxiety and allows you to follow the shot sequence.

Training your breathing

You can increase your **lung capacity** primarily through fitness training and improve your oxygen absorption. You will be more efficient and have more endurance.

During training you should also learn to better control your **anxiety**. If you are very anxious and barely able to concentrate, targeted breathing will calm you down. But if you are lacking the necessary anxiety for a competition you can generate the critical excitement and alertness with special breathing exercises.

Belly breathing

You can choose to use belly breathing or chest breathing. However, belly breathing is recommended for the rifle shooter because it allows you to absorb more oxygen and better control your anxiety. Deep belly breathing lowers your center of gravity, which is more conducive to a stable firing position.

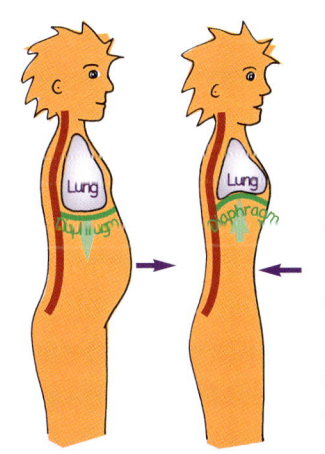

- As you inhale your stomach pushes out and as you exhale it pushes inward.
- The air is inhaled and exhaled primarily through the movement of the diaphragm.
- Lung capacity is better utilized.
- The shoulders barely move.

Training Shooting Sports

Breathing during the shot sequence

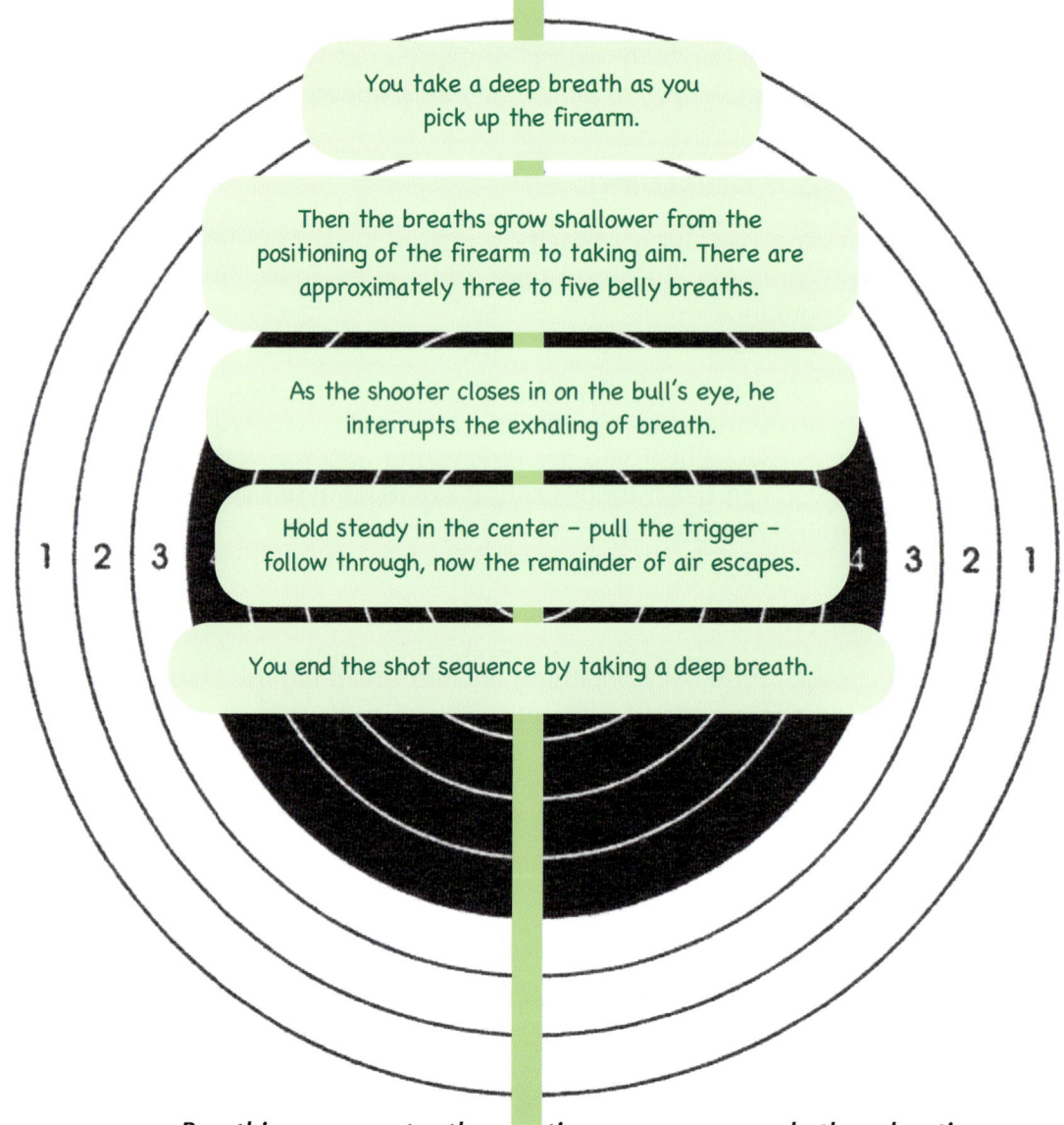

You take a deep breath as you pick up the firearm.

Then the breaths grow shallower from the positioning of the firearm to taking aim. There are approximately three to five belly breaths.

As the shooter closes in on the bull's eye, he interrupts the exhaling of breath.

Hold steady in the center – pull the trigger – follow through, now the remainder of air escapes.

You end the shot sequence by taking a deep breath.

Breathing supports the motion sequence and the shooting technique. You should find your own, always consistent breathing rhythm. That means: same number of breaths, same force and same frequency. With this routine you will be better able to maintain your shot rhythm.

Pistol Shooting

...... 9 Pistol Shooting

Its many different disciplines make pistol shooting one of the most diverse firearm sports. For many people the fascination is based on the mastery of a hand-held firearm. It is fired with the same hand that holds it.

The Olympic rifle disciplines include:

	Men	Women
Air pistol	60 shots	40 shots
Free pistol	60 shots	-
Small bore sport pistol	-	30 + 30 shots
Rapid fire pistol	2 x 30 shots	-

You can find a list of events for all age groups, regional and national competitions as well as regulations on the National Rifle Association's website (www.usashooting.com for the US and www.nsra.co.uk for the UK). International competitions are conducted according to the ISSF, the international umbrella organization.

Training Shooting Sports

Firing position procedure

The object of the firing position is to make both body and firearm as stable as possible. To do so you must have a balanced stance, a low center of gravity and the right amount of muscle tension.

External firing position refers to the body's visible position: feet, body, arms and head. This is also the order in which the firing position is established.

Internal firing position refers to the state of muscular tension, the stretching of ligaments and the position of the parts of the body relative to each other. This is hardly visible from the outside but you can sense it with your "muscle sense".

Foot position

- The feet are about shoulder-width apart.
- The feet are parallel to each other.
- Weight is equally distributed over the soles of both feet.
- The knees are locked.
- Wobbles can be balanced by slightly turning the toes in or out.

Body position

- The upper body is erect and the hips are square.
- The weight is equally distributed over both legs and feet.
- Your center of gravity lies in the area between your feet.

Pistol Shooting

Arm position

The free arm is fixed at the waistband or in the pants or jacket pocket.

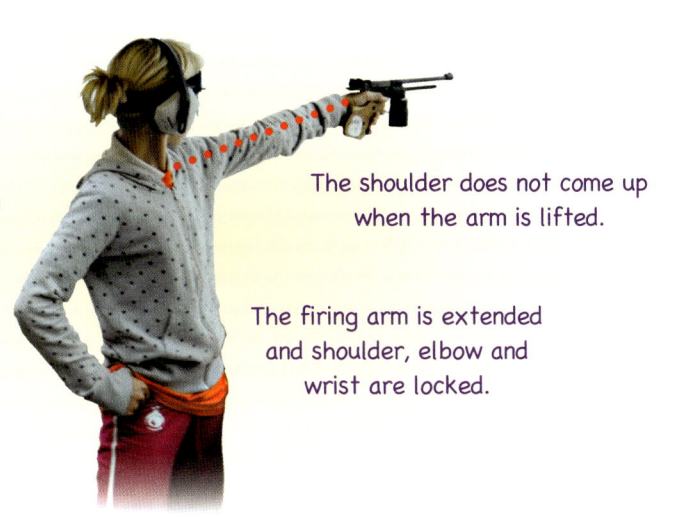

The shoulder does not come up when the arm is lifted.

The firing arm is extended and shoulder, elbow and wrist are locked.

Head position

- The head is held erect and straight.
- You turn your head toward the target only so far as your neck muscles will allow without tensing up.
- As a right-handed shooter you can see just above the sight line with your right eye.
- To maintain an even sight line you must make sure that your head position is consistent.

Firearm position

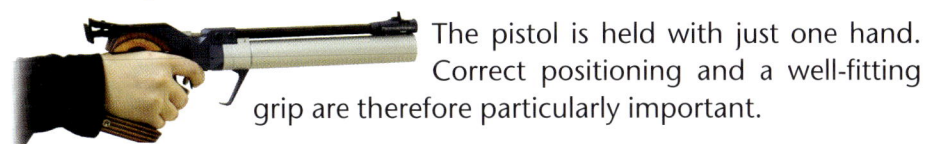

The pistol is held with just one hand. Correct positioning and a well-fitting grip are therefore particularly important.

- The free hand places the firearm in the cradle between index finger and thumb.
- Now place the pad of your first phalanx of the index finger on the middle of the trigger lever.
- Next your fingers and palm wrap around the grip.
- The thumb lies on the thumb rest without pressure.

An individually adjusted or customized grip allows the hand to hold the pistol evenly.

Training Shooting Sports

Setting up and checking the firing position

When setting up at the shooting stand, the firing position must be aligned with the bull's eye. **You can do this the following way:**

- You guide the firearm below the bull's eye into the aiming area and stop there.
- Now lower your gaze without moving your head while breathing slowly.
- Now shift your gaze back to the front sight and check to see if your firearm's position in the aiming area has changed.
- In case of deviations you must make the appropriate corrections.

Right angle firing position

The ideal firing position for a pistol shooter is the right angle firing position. This gives you the best sight line of eye-rear sight-front sight-bull's eye, and the body absorbs the recoil from the small bore pistol straight on.

- The feet are parallel.
- The shoulder joint is an extension of the sight line.
- The head is turned hard to the shoulder.

Open firing position

If the physical qualifications are not right for the right angle firing position, the angle can be adjusted slightly.

- The shoulder joint obliquely faces in the shooting direction.
- The angle of the feet to the line of fire is smaller than 90°.

Pistol Shooting

Motion sequence and technical elements

The motion sequence for precision shooting can be divided into five phases:

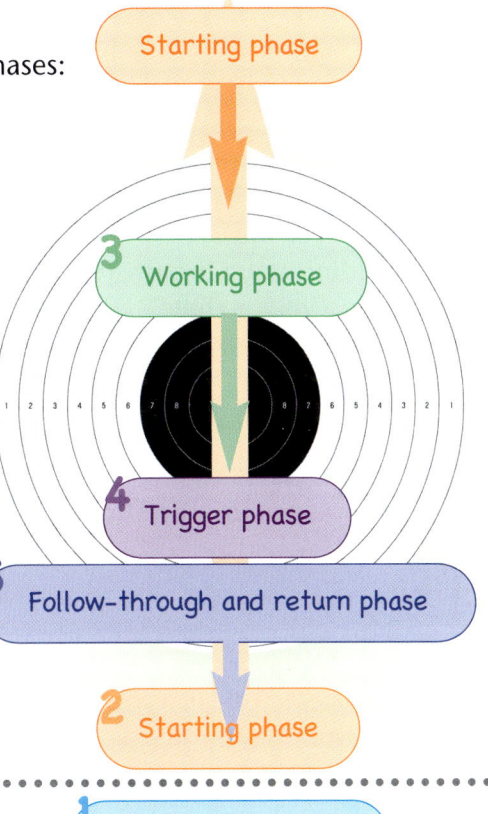

- **3** Working phase
- **4** Trigger phase
- **5** Follow-through and return phase
- **2** Starting phase
- **1** Preparation phase

1 Preparation phase

During this phase you mentally prepare yourself for the impending task. In doing so you **take several deliberate breaths**, lock your elbow and wrist and build up muscle tension in your body. Your gaze is unfocused – **resting gaze**. You always put your index finger in the same spot on the lever.

2 Starting phase

You begin by taking a **deep breath** (belly breathing) as you raise the firearm to just above the target. At the turning point the firearm briefly comes to a rest. To take **approximate aim** the front sight is centered in the rear sight notch. With the **first calm exhalation** you move the firearm to the center of the white above the bull's eye. Your **gaze is on the rear sight or the back of the hand**.

115

Training Shooting Sports

You hold your breath for a moment as you steady the firearm and find the **pressure point** and check the front sight and rear sight notch.

3 Working phase

The firearm is not raised again with the second inhalation (belly breathing). After **holding your breath for several moments**, you **exhale very slowly** (two-way breathing) and slowly lower the firearm through the middle of the bull's eye to the **aiming area**.

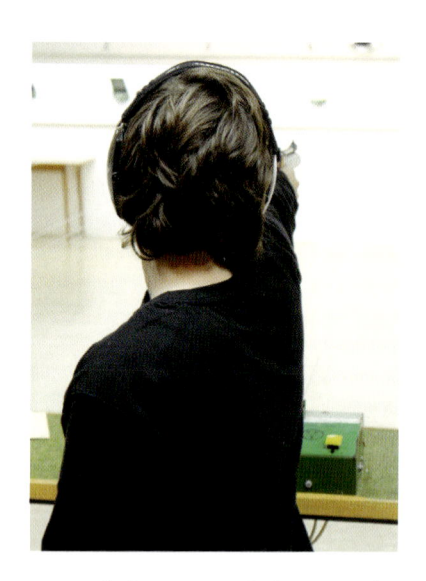

Next you locate the **front sight in the center of the rear sight notch**. Increase **pressure on the trigger**.

4 Trigger phase

Once you have reached the aiming area you stop breathing. You do not **breathe for several seconds** and your **firearm comes to a rest**. Your eye locates the front sight and if the sight picture is perfect, the **shot is released**.

If you are not able to release the shot within five seconds, you should abort.

5 Follow-through and return phase

After the shot is released the **muscle tension remains** and you continue to hold the firearm **in firing position**. Your gaze stays on the front sight and you do **not breathe**. Where were the sights at the moment the shot was fired?

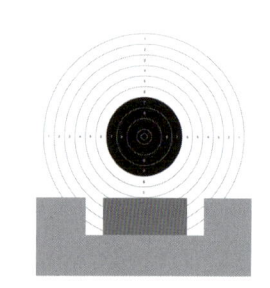

You **breathe again** as the firearm returns, the eye can follow the front sight and the **muscle tension is released**.

Pistol Shooting

Breathing

Breathing supplies you with the necessary oxygen that allows your brain, muscles and sensory organs to work at their best. Deliberate breathing also facilitates your shooting technique and helps control excessive or insufficient anxiety. We chose to describe two-way breathing here because it is what the advanced shooters use.

If you cannot hold the pistol for very long just yet it would be better to start with one-way breathing. Ask your trainer about it!

The illustration of the two-way breathing technique (1, 2) shows the progression of inhalation (high curve) and exhalation (low curve) during a shot.

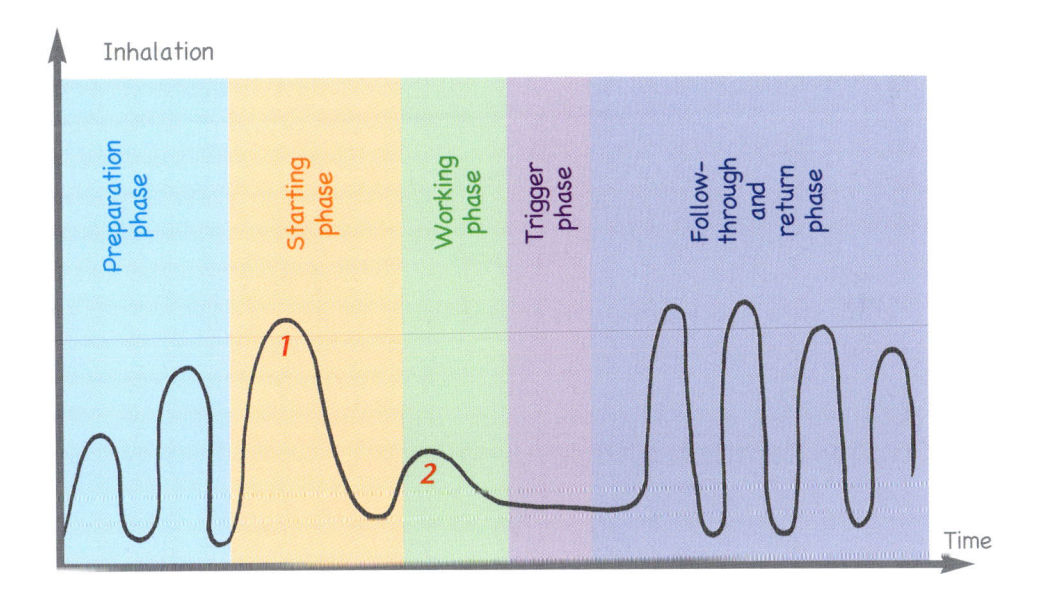

During the individual shooting phases, breathing either stops partially or slows down. It is therefore very important that the shooter inhales and exhales deeply after firing or aborting a shot. That's how you refill your oxygen tank!

Training Shooting Sports

Control of breathing motion

Inhale deeply as you raise the firearm.

After holding your breath for a moment, slowly exhale and lower the firearm to the target.

The firearm comes to a rest during a period of no breathing.

The firearm does not move during a deep inhalation.

The air slowly flows out after briefly holding it in. The exhalation defines the downward motion into the aiming area.

Exhalation stops in the aiming area. The firearm comes to a rest.

The shot is released during an extended no breathing period.

After the shot, the no breathing period extends into the follow-through.

After briefly inhaling and exhaling deeply, the shooter resumes normal breathing.

Breathing facilitates the motion sequence and the shooting technique. The breathing rhythm remains the same throughout the process and is individually adapted by the shooter.

Pistol Shooting

Anxiety control

When you are shooting (particularly in a competition) you want to be relaxed, alert, calm and focused. This ideal state isn't always easy to achieve because you are affected by everyday life and the competitive situation.

High anxiety

- You are very agitated and are afraid of failing.
- Loud noises, shouts or conversations make you nervous and angry.
- Poor interim results really upset you.
- …

You need to take soothing breaths! Deliberately slow down your exhalation!

Low anxiety

- You are tired and don't feel fit.
- A poor interim result makes you sad and discouraged.
- You are exhausted from the long competition day.
- …

You need stimulating breathing! Deliberately emphasize inhalation!

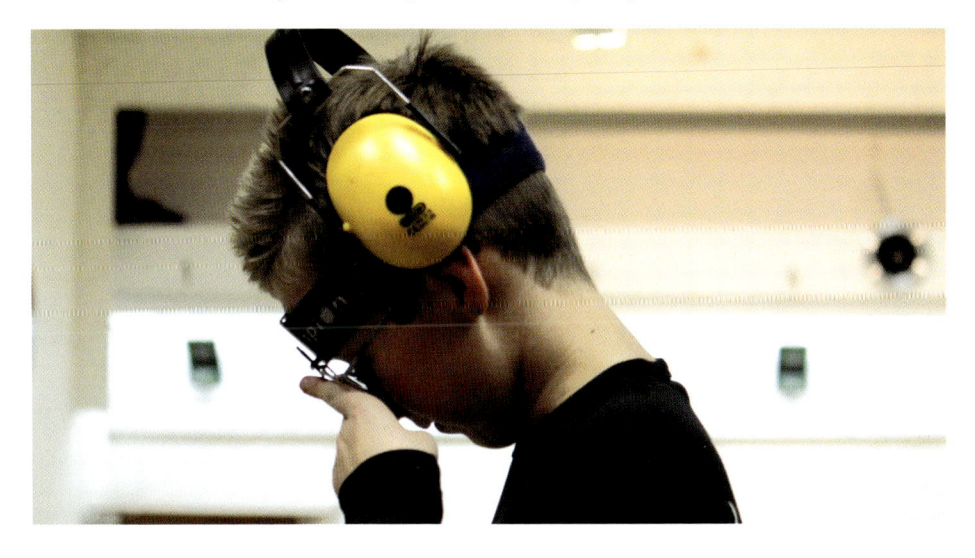

Training Shooting Sports

General yoga breathing to calm yourself

When you are very anxious your breathing is faster and your heart rate is higher. This has a negative effect on your aiming. You can collect yourself by doing some simple breathing techniques.

Alternate nostril breathing

- *The right index finger and middle finger touch the base of your nose.*
- *The thumb covers the right nostril and you slowly exhale through the left nostril. Then the breath flows back in.*
- *Now release the thumb.*
- *The pinky covers the left nostril and you slowly exhale through the right nostril. Afterwards you let the air flow back in.*
- *Release the pinky and switch again.*

Belly breathing

You lie flat and relaxed on a not-too-soft surface. Set a small object such as a stuffed animal on your stomach. As you take calm belly breaths you can watch the object gently move up and down or slowly rock back and forth.

The clam

You lie on your back and your knees are bent.

- As you inhale your knees fall open and arms and hands spread at your sides, – "the clam opens!"
- As you exhale "the clam closes!" The knees slowly come together and the arms move back toward the body.

Pistol Shooting

General yoga breathing to "wake up"

If you are tired and unmotivated you can put yourself into the necessary "working mode" for shooting by doing some targeted breathing exercises.

Ha breathing

Shallow breathing often leaves too much stale air behind in the lungs. This causes headaches, lack in motivation and lack of concentration. Now the lungs must be "cleansed"!

- You stand with your feet slightly apart and exhale.
- As you inhale you extend your arms up on either side of the head and clasp your hands.
- Gently bend your upper body back briefly and then drop the upper body and arms forward.
- As you do so exhale with a big "Ha!"
- Your legs are straight, the upper body hangs loosely and the arms swing between your legs.

HAAAAAA...!

UAAAH...!

Gorilla breath

With his characteristic gesture the gorilla seeks courage and gathers strength. Try it out!

- In a standing position inhale deeply through the nose.
- As you exhale pound your fists against your chest and roar "Uuuah"!
- Be aware of your surroundings! Maybe the roar needs to be a little quieter.

You can find additional breathing exercises in the book "Learning Shooting Sports", pg. 46/47. Your trainer will show you another special breathing technique for "adjusting up and down" in an actual competitive situation!

Training Shooting Sports

Aiming

When taking aim you point the firearm at the target with help from your eye and the sights in such a way that you will hit the center of the target as accurately as possible. Rear sight and front sight are the sighting elements, and the imaginary line from eye to rear sight to front sight to target is called the sight line.

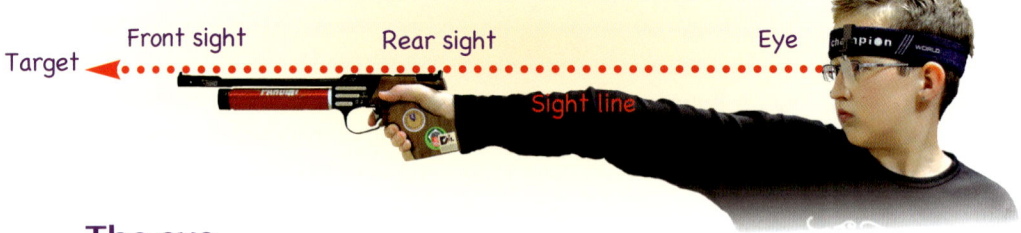

The eye

The eye plays a very important role in the aiming process. That is why you have to follow certain rules.

Dominant eye

You take aim at the target with just one eye, your dominant eye. The other eye remains open but covered with a translucent eye blind. This way both eyes have the same incidence of light. The right eye is the preferred aiming eye for right-handed shooters.

Light and dark

The pupil of your eye reacts to changing incidence of light. It contracts if there is a lot of light and dilates in darkness (here bright sunlight and subsequent look at the dark center of the target). Because the pupil requires a relatively long time to adjust to a change in light conditions you should avoid extreme changes just before taking aim. It would make focusing much more difficult.

It's best to wear a cap or a headband with a visor.

Pistol Shooting

Keen vision

When objects are different distances away (here rear sight, front sight, target), the eye can only see one of them in sharp focus. That is why all of the focus is on the front sight. But since the eye can see the front sight clearly for only a short time the shot should be released after about five seconds or the aiming process should be stopped and repeated. Aiming mistakes can be avoided this way.

Eyesight

You should have your vision checked at regular intervals. If a visual impairment is detected you can balance it with optical lenses.

Aiming phases

There are different sight pictures during the aiming process.

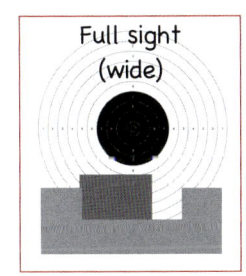

Full sight (wide)	Full sight (high)	Fine sight (low)	Correct sight picture Half sight
The front sight is within the rear sight, but fixed on the left.	The light bars are equally wide but the front sight is above the line.	The light bars have the same width but the front sight is below the line.	The light bars have the same width and the front and rear sights are lined up!

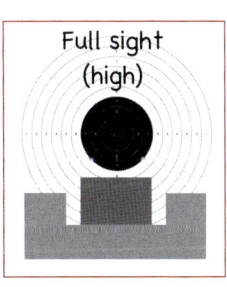

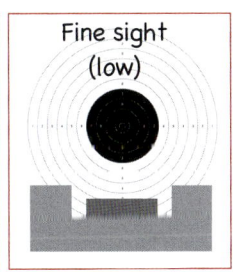

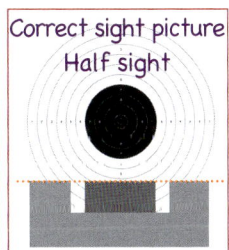

Training Shooting Sports

The aiming process

Before raising the firearm your gaze is relaxed and unfocused.

As you raise the firearm your gaze shifts to the base of the hand, to the sights at the return point, and you bring the front sight into the center of the rear sight notch. **Full sight**

During the lowering motion your eyes rest on the base of the hand or the rear sight, without actually fixing your eyes on it.

During the extended non-breathing period you check to see if the front sight is in the center of the rear sight. **Full sight**

From here onward keep your eye on the sights, initially without fixating them.

During the downward motion into the aiming area your focus is on the front sight.

Focus on the front sight as you move across the bull's eye. **Fine sight**

Once you reach the aiming area you do not blink and you continue to focus on the front sight. **Final aim**

When you have the perfect sight picture, release the shot!

During the follow-through phase your eyes stay on the front sight.

The final aim phase should not take longer than five seconds, and then the shot should break. If not, you should abort!

Pistol Shooting

Pulling the trigger

When the perfect sight picture has been achieved, you release the shot.

- As you pull the trigger you increase pressure on the lever so the firearm stays in place as the shot breaks.
- The first phalanx of your index finger pushes straight down on the center of the trigger lever.

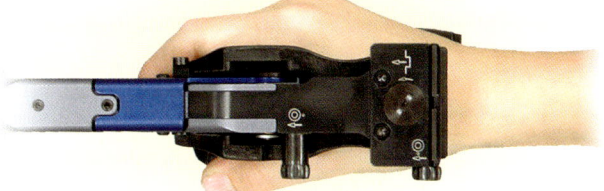

Trigger slack and pressure point

The air pistol as well as the sport pistol trigger is adjusted with a pressure point. There is a slack weight and a pull weight.

Adjustment

The ratio of slack weight to pull weight can be adjusted individually. The standard is: 2/3 to 1/3. Try it out! **Pull weight regulations** are specified in the CMP/NRA and ISSF competition rulebooks. The pull weight for the **air pistol** is **500 grams**.

The pressure point setting must be such that you can feel it and hold it properly even under shooting match conditions.

Training Shooting Sports

Pressure progression

During the *preparation phase* you always put your finger in the same spot on the lever.

As you inhale the *finger is actively placed on the lever.*

You find the *pressure point* with the first exhalation (no later than the extended non-breathing phase).

You *hold the pressure* or increase it slightly with the second inhalation.

You actively *increase the pressure* as you move across the target, to about 80% to 90% of the pull weight.

You continue to increase pressure in the *aiming area* until you achieve the perfect sight picture and *release the shot.*

After the *shot is released* and during the follow-through phase your finger slowly returns to the *starting position*, but it maintains *contact* with the trigger lever.

In the beginning, try not to find the pressure point too quickly, and release the shot with sensitivity.

Pistol Shooting

Sport pistol duel shooting

After having focused exclusively on static precision firing as it applies to air pistol as well as free pistol and the **first half course for** sport pistol, we should go a step further and briefly introduce the duel shooting technique.

> ### The second half course for sport pistol consists of:
> - **Six series** of **five shots** each.
> - In a rhythm of **seven-second breaks** and **three seconds for shooting, five shots** are fired respectively.

Firing position set-up

The firing position is not too different from the described precision firing position. Here are a few differences:

- The stance can be slightly wider.
- The firearm is held more firmly since the pistol must be continuously raised and lowered and cannot slip from the receiver.
- Raising and lowering the arm with the weight of the pistol can easily cause the body to sway and therefore necessitates more muscle tension.

Head position

The same rules apply for the head position as in precision shooting.

Training Shooting Sports

Body position / arm position

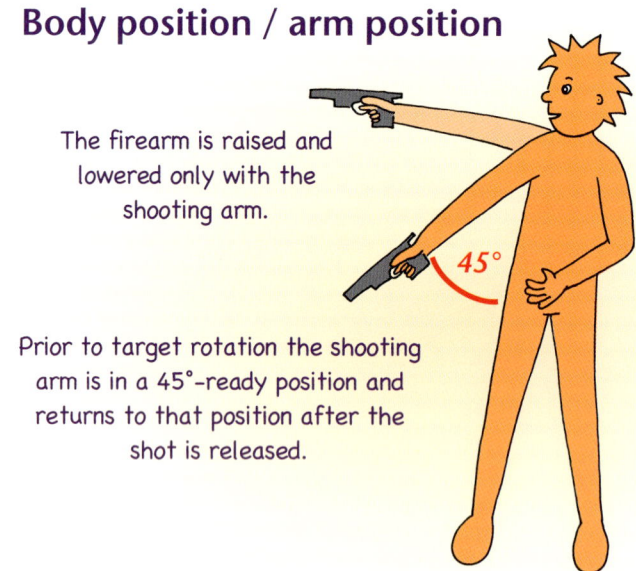

The firearm is raised and lowered only with the shooting arm.

During the raising and lowering, the angle from the shoulder line to the shooting arm always remains the same.

45°

Prior to target rotation the shooting arm is in a 45°-ready position and returns to that position after the shot is released.

Upper body and hips remain fixed during arm movement.

Motion sequence

The duel shooting motion sequence is divided into six phases:

1. Preparation phase
One minute to load the firearm, assume the 45°-ready position, find the pressure point.

2. Reaction phase
The time period between target rotation and the arm being raised.

3. Acceleration phase
The firearm is raised quickly.

4. Deceleration phase
The firearm is slowed down.

5. Release phase
The firearm stays in the aiming area until the shot breaks.

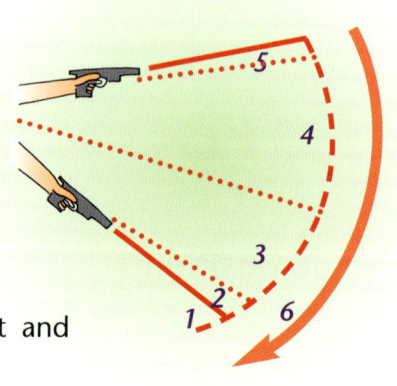

6. Follow-through and return phase
The firearm stays in place after the shot and then is returned to starting position. Breathing technique.

Pistol Shooting

The breathing technique paces the motion sequence:

- You slowly exhale upon the command "Attention!" and guide the firearm into ready position.
- You await the target rotation or the green light with exhaled breath.
- You inhale as you raise the arm and hold the firearm in the aiming area.
- You slowly exhale after firing and the follow through and lower your firearm.
- During the seven-second break you take one to two deep breaths. Here your breathing serves as a timer!
- This sequence is repeated five times. After the five-shot series the oxygen deficit is corrected through more intensive breathing.

Aiming

For aiming the same basic rules apply as for the precision technique, but the sight picture looks slightly different. The target is very different from a precision target. The aiming area in duel shooting is in the lower part of the bull's eye centered between the two white light bars. The lines are visually positioned on top of the sights. A narrow black space is visible between the sights and the lines.

Here too, the eye focuses on the front sight. In the ready position the front sight is not yet visible in the rear sight (fine sight). During the upward movement the fine sight changes to full sight (the wrist is fixed!).

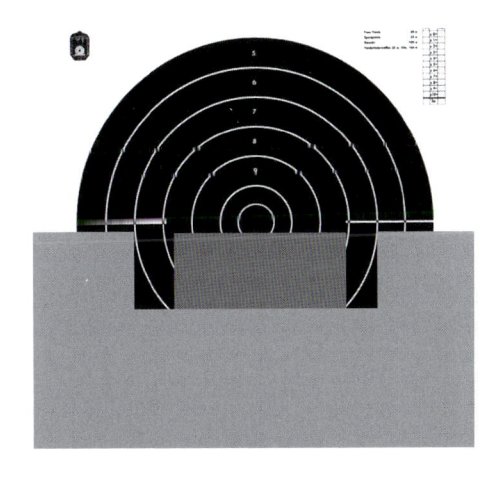

Training Shooting Sports

Pulling the trigger

To pull the trigger the same simple ground rules apply as in the precision technique. The pressure point is actively located approximately two seconds before target rotation during the preparation phase. As the firearm is raised the pressure is increased so the shot can break as soon as the perfect sight picture has been detected after reaching the aiming area. The pressure is maintained during the follow-through, and then the finger returns to the starting position.

........10 Safety First!

Many great and useful things in this world also harbor a certain amount of danger if they are not handled properly. We must learn to work with sharp knives in the kitchen, to safely navigate traffic in cars, and fencers put on protective gear and wear a mask before they fence.

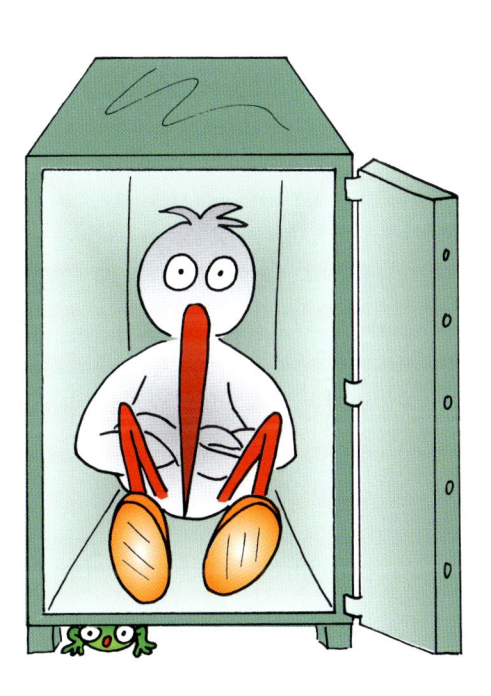

Firearms are not without danger. That makes it all the more important for young athletes to be introduced to and be made familiar with the safety rules. When someone joins a club he must first prove that he is responsible and careful and doesn't just randomly fire in all directions, but rather understands the sport and is willing to learn everything that is important. That is why there is a lot of preparatory training, people use laser light pistols or rifles, and adolescents shoot primarily with air guns.

Sports firearms are safe pieces of sports equipment, but only if the athletes know how to use them and obey all of the safety rules!

Training Shooting Sports

Safekeeping

The purchase and possession of sports firearms as well as their transportation to training and competition sites are subject to **gun control laws**. Sports firearms and ammunition must be stored in such a way as to prevent loss or access by unauthorized third persons. This is done at the club as well as the home with *special safes*.

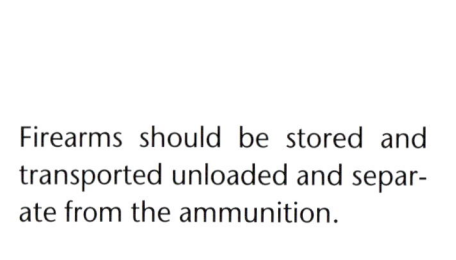

Firearms should be stored and transported unloaded and separate from the ammunition.

Shooting operation

Children and adolescents under the age of 18 operating air firearms or other firearms must be supervised at all times by a parent or another authorized adult, or a certified range safety officer.

Shooting and range safety supervision

Shooting ranges have one or more safety officers on duty. All shooters must register with the range safety officer before any firearm is uncased. Shooters must obey all commands from the range safety officer, staff or attendants.

Safety First!

Important regulations in shooting sports

All shooting athletes must obey current safety regulations. This is very important to ensure fair competitions and the utmost safety at the shooting range.

The National Rifle Association has compiled a list of general safety rules as well as special safety rules for individual disciplines.

They focus on:
- Safety
- Equipment and firearm inspection
- Competition procedure and scoring
- Scheduling and submission
- Titles and records

During the firearms inspection the sports equipment is checked for compliance with the specifications and visibly approved for competition with a sticker.

Training Shooting Sports

Safety First!

Safety at the shooting range

Safety at the shooting range is extremely important, which is why there must be strict rules. It is the only way to guarantee a safe and fair competition.

Here are some excerpts from the NRA safety rules:

1. Always keep the gun pointed in a safe direction!
2. Always keep your finger off the trigger until ready to shoot!
3. Always keep the gun unloaded until ready to use!
4. Know your target and what is beyond!
5. Use only the correct ammunition for your gun!
6. Use eye and ear protection as appropriate!
7. Know how to use the gun safely!
8. Be sure your gun is safe to operate!
9. Never use alcohol, over-the-counter prescription or other drugs before or while shooting!
10. Store your guns so they are not accessible to unauthorized persons!
11. Pay attention!
12. Regularly clean your firearm!
13. Be aware that certain types of guns and many shooting activities require additional safety precautions!
14. Always keep the safety on when not shooting!
15. Do not pick up a gun and point it down range while other shooters are setting up targets!

You can look up all the US-rules on the NRA website at www.nrahq.org or request a brochure. For the UK, please go to www.nsra.co.uk. Safety rules are always updated. Ask your trainer about it!

Training Shooting Sports

Against firearm misuse

In recent years there have been isolated but terrifying incidents of adolescents obtaining a firearm to shoot fellow students and teachers. These rampages caused much sorrow and have left fear in their wake.

It is very important to find out why this happens and what can be done about it. In the search for reasons and causes, focus has repeatedly been on the shooting athlete, although one has nothing to do with the other.

Shooting athletes should help to eliminate prejudices and prevent such catastrophes.

What can be done against firearm misuse?

- *You have to be vigilant.*
-
-
-
-
-

What are your ideas? Talk about it with your training buddies and trainer. Here is a place for you to record them.

Cooperation is needed

As a young shooting athlete it certainly isn't always easy to confidently defend your sport to others. There are many preconceptions and plenty of people associate shooting sports with violence and danger.

The way you talk about your sport, your appearance and the way you handle yourself as a shooting athlete can make a positive or negative public impression.

Shooting athletes should make clear how much emphasis is put on safety in shooting sports and especially clarify how much shooting athletes appreciate their responsibilities.

Arguments for shooting sports

- *Shooting sports teach you to work with rules.*
-
-
-
-
-
-

What are your arguments? Talk about it with your training buddies and your trainer. Here is a place for you to record them.

Training Shooting Sports

O	P	R	M	P	O	T	A	T	O	E	S	E	B
Z	U	C	C	H	I	N	I	W	L	T	M	R	I
S	V	N	M	Y	L	M	S	C	I	W	O	T	X
Q	D	M	G	Y	R	O	C	I	H	C	W	F	Z
U	M	R	E	B	M	U	C	U	C	Y	U	O	I
A	N	A	P	R	T	Y	M	O	W	O	K	T	H
S	X	N	W	S	G	V	L	R	N	M	P	A	C
H	I	A	V	K	G	I	Y	U	C	X	W	F	A
P	I	N	A	P	P	L	E	M	S	E	Z	M	N
S	N	A	R	W	H	L	E	T	T	U	C	E	I
K	Z	B	P	E	P	P	E	R	S	K	T	W	P
P	E	A	R	W	C	A	R	R	O	T	L	S	S
G	R	A	P	E	S	W	F	L	E	M	O	N	I
K	I	W	I	Y	R	R	E	B	W	A	R	T	S

Fruits and vegetables are healthy!

Find 17 fruits and vegetables – horizontally, vertically or diagonally, forwards and backwards!

Oh Dear!
Always such excitement before a competition!

Which is the quickest way to the restroom?

Can you trace the route?

Tom asks his friend: "How high is the barrier?"
The friend climbs to the top and shouts: "Fourteen feet!"
Says Tom: "You're so dumb!
You could have waited until the barrier comes down!" Answers his friend: "But I wanted to measure how high it is and not how wide!"

138

Fit and Healthy

..... 11 Fit and Healthy

Anyone who thinks that training hard several times a week is enough for athletic success will soon learn the better. Next to the demanding training, periods of recuperation are very important; also plenty of sleep, good nutrition, physical hygiene, organization and much more.

You should learn to listen to your body. It tells you when you are particularly fit or when you urgently need rest and should relax. A good shooting athlete has a healthy diet and drinks plenty of fluids to stay efficient and focused.

In this chapter we have compiled some interesting information on this topic. Take this as an incentive to learn more about your body and good nutrition.

Have fun!

Our performance capacity

In the course of a day our performance capacity experiences highs and lows, as you can see on the curve below. This is similar for all people, and we have adjusted our lives accordingly. Most school instruction is done in the morning, then some people even take a nap during lunch, in the afternoon we accelerate again, and at night our body gets its well-earned sleep. Anyone who follows this rhythm lives a healthy and productive life. You can feel it if you don't get enough rest and sufficient sleep, and it would be a shame not to utilize those physical "highs".

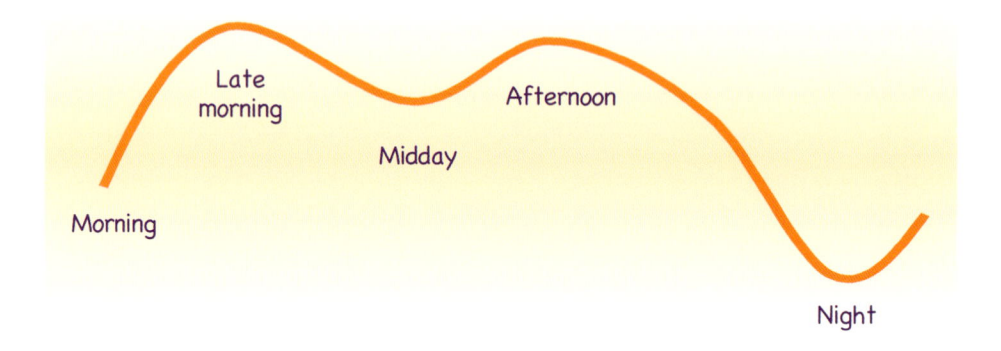

Eat and drink yourself fit

Athletes who eat or drink too much or the wrong things before training are not efficient. They feel stuffed and appear tired and listless. Many body functions slow down because the stomach is working overtime. But we must eat and especially drink to replenish the body's used up energy and to balance the loss of fluids caused by sweating. It is also necessary to do so periodically during long training sessions and competitions.

Look at this overview to see what is suitable for your main meals, snacks, and the in between energy boost, and what isn't. Choose your foods and drinks, as well as the time of consumption so you are sufficiently satiated during training or at a tournament, but are not still digesting.

Fit and Healthy

How long foods stay in the stomach until they are digested:

Approx. one hour: Water, tea, broth.
Approx. 2 – 3 hours: Cocoa, banana, apple, roll, rice, cooked fish, soft boiled egg, whole grain bread.
Approx. 4 – 5 hours: Sausage, meat, fried potatoes, French fries, beans or peas.
Approx. 6- 7 hours: Layer-cake, mushrooms, fish in oil, fatty roast.

Don't forget to drink!

To balance the loss of fluids from sweating you have to drink enough fluids during training and competition. When choosing fluids pay attention to important minerals such as potassium, calcium or magnesium.

- **Suitable beverages before and during exertion**
  Water, juice and water mix in proportions of approximately 1:3, lightly sweetened fruit tea. Don't choose beverages that are really cold because the body has to expend lots of energy to warm it up.

- **Suitable beverages after exertion**
  Juice and water mix with a higher juice ratio, beverages with higher sugar content.

Training Shooting Sports

Energy sources

You are only capable of extreme physical exertion if you intake sufficient energy (sugar/starch) in the form of nourishment. If you have absorbed a sufficient amount you achieve optimal performance capacity. Not enough causes a drop in efficiency, lack of concentration and fatigue. But with too much energy absorption there is a danger of extreme nervousness and quick exhaustion.

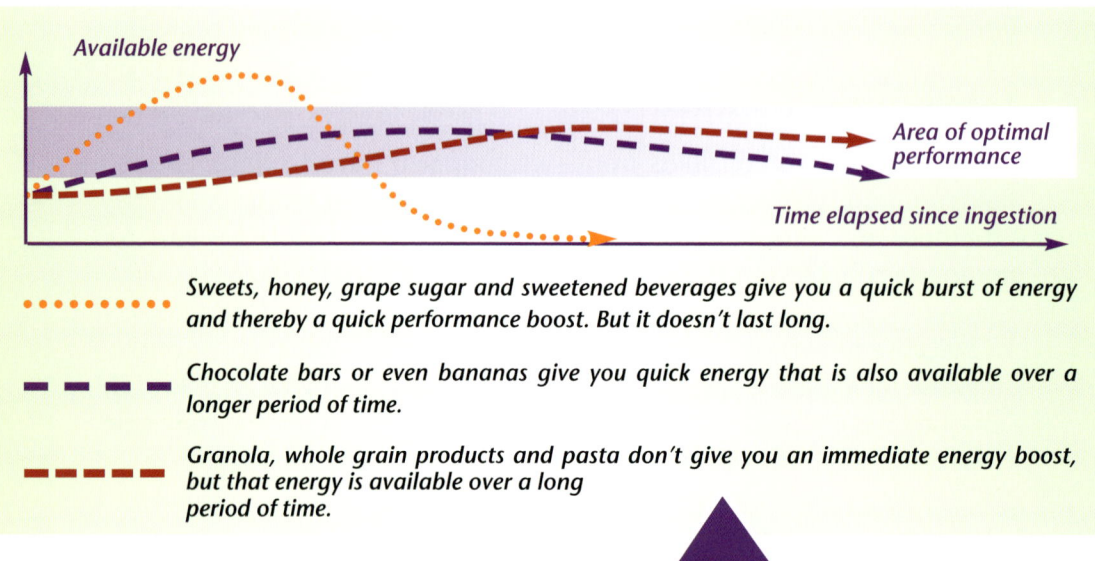

Available energy

Area of optimal performance

Time elapsed since ingestion

.... Sweets, honey, grape sugar and sweetened beverages give you a quick burst of energy and thereby a quick performance boost. But it doesn't last long.

– – – Chocolate bars or even bananas give you quick energy that is also available over a longer period of time.

– – – Granola, whole grain products and pasta don't give you an immediate energy boost, but that energy is available over a long period of time.

The **food pyramid** shows which foods you should eat in large quantities (very bottom) and which you should preferably eat very rarely (very top). Examples are given for each food group.

Cake, cookies, chocolate, candy

Milk, cheese, yogurt, sausage, meat, eggs, beans, peas, nuts

Bananas, apples, oranges, kiwi, carrots, tomatoes, salad, broccoli, cucumbers, peppers

Bread, potatoes, rice, noodles, Muesli, cornflakes

Water, juice and water mix, tea, whey

Fit and Healthy

Prevention and regeneration

Warming up and mobilizing

To prevent injuries and overload damages you should prepare your body for the impending strain. Warming up and doing flexibility exercises are particularly important before jogging or playing sports, and limbering-up, mobilization and reaction exercises are important before shooting practice. Since you need a certain amount of muscle tension for the individual firing positions, you should avoid flexibility exercises right before shooting as these decrease muscle tone and the feel for the muscle tension is lost.

Rest and regeneration

After a strenuous run or a sports game, it is important to do a calm and slow cool down to gently allow the cardiovascular system to recover. But the pulse also races at shooting sports competitions. Such a competition is an enormous strain on muscles, heart, circulation and the nervous system. Here, too, running or walking is an ideal method for "blowing off steam" and clearing the mind. It allows the body to recuperate and build up reserves for impending strain.

Training the immune system

Due to the resulting exhaustion, athletic strain puts the body in a temporarily vulnerable position that makes it more prone to catching colds. To avoid susceptibility to viruses that promote colds, you should take the necessary precautions and specifically train for temperature tolerance.

- Do not let the body get cold after physical strain (warm functional clothing).
- After perspiring take a luke-warm shower, vigorously towel off and nurture your body.
- Balance loss of fluids by drinking properly (see page 141).
- Occasionally use a sauna or steam bath and take alternating hot and cold showers or footbaths after getting up in the morning.

Training Shooting Sports

United against doping

Being a winner is a great feeling! You're on cloud nine, everyone is proud of you and you see the reward for all your hard work. It is really fun and should just go on and on …!

But there can be moments of crisis:

- You think you have reached the limits of your performance capacity.
- You work really hard and still have no success.
- You are afraid your competitors are using illegal substances and want to counteract that unfairness.
- Your trainer or your parents expect more from you but you feel that you are not capable of more at the moment.
- You feel that you were judged unfairly by the event judges.
- You are fighting for a spot on the shooting squad.
- You have a long-term injury that just won't heal.

Resist the temptation to reach for illegal substances!

- Doping damages your body!
- Doping is fraud!
- Doping threatens the sport!

The U.S. Anti-Doping Agency (USADA) and UK Anti-Doping (UKAD) work to protect the health of athletes by deterring the use of performance-enhancing substances and to preserve sport for clean athletes through education and resources.

Get timely information and seek advice

If you are stuck and need advice, talk to your parents, you trainer or other trusted individuals. In this training book for young shooting athletes you will find many suggestions for goal-oriented training, for dealing with pressure and defeat, and how you can calm yourself and focus without the use of illegal substances. You can also find lots of information an all of the above topics on the internet or in magazines.

Fit and Healthy

Advice from Claudia Bokel

Claudia Bokel is a member of the advisory committee for active athletes in the German Olympic Sports Association (DOSB), a world and European champion in epee fencing, chairwoman of the EOC and member of the IOC Athlete's Commission, and a committee member of the World Anti-doping Agency (WADA).

"I think the anti-doping movement is good because it is important for every young athlete to know everything that has to do with doping. I think it's great that the anti-doping movement helps you – the young athletes – to take a stand against doping, that it helps you to defend yourselves whenever you are confronted with this issue. Sports can be so much fun even if there are low points. Defeat is not pleasant but it is part of the sport. I learned that when I was very young. And once you have overcome defeat you can be proud, but only if you overcome it without doping! Doping does not make you proud but rather is a great threat to sports."

Many other top athletes also continue to speak out against doping and for fairness in sports. Join them by not giving doping a chance!

Training Shooting Sports

Have you ever tried to look at a target without the "ring number counter" in your eyes? Just as individual stars form the signs of the zodiac, so do bullet holes form images on the target. Try it!

146

Solutions

............12 Solutions

Pg. 73 **Our opinion:**
Self confidence – enjoy training – ~~self-doubt~~ – ~~blind rage~~ – willingness to take risks – ~~impatience~~ – being laid-back – ~~fear of making mistakes~~ – ambition – desire to win – faith in one's performance – ~~fear of failure~~ – ~~bad mood~~ – feeling in great form – attentiveness – concentration – ~~cockiness.~~

Pg. 76/77 **15-18 points**
You can go far with your attitude to the sport. You enjoy competition, are fair and are able to conquer your weaker self. Keep it up!

10-14 points
You have a pretty good attitude to the sport but you sometimes drive only in first gear. With a more fun and competitive spirit you could be more successful. Take the training and competitions seriously and treat the other athletes fairly.

6-9 points
You are not particularly ambitious and think mostly about yourself! You need to work on your attitude about performance and team spirit.

Pg. 78

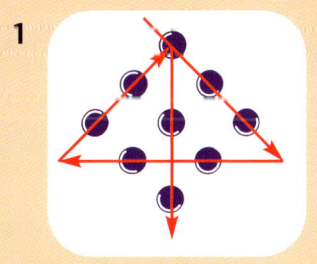

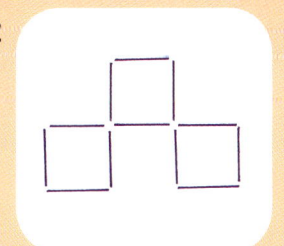

3 Unfortunately the little bug does not reach his true love.
4 There are 35 triangles.

Training Shooting Sports

Pg. 138

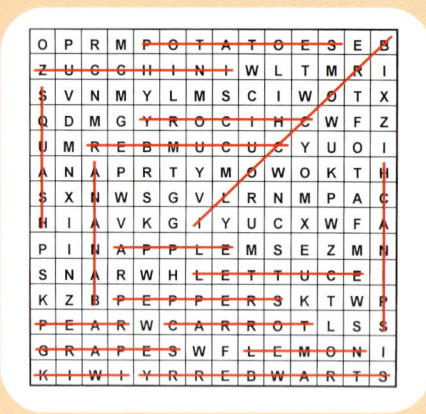

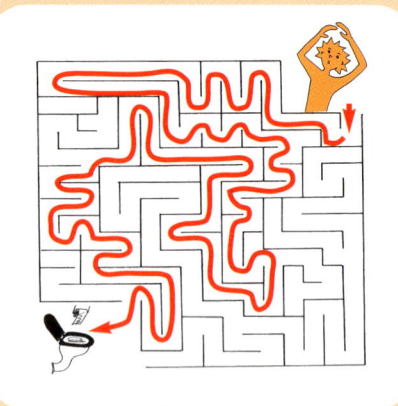

13 Let's Talk

Dear Parents,

At an age when many children play soccer, take ballet lessons or swim, your child has decided to become a shooting athlete. So what makes this sport so special? It is not size, strength, beauty or elegance that matter in shooting sports, but rather focus, determination, good judgment and resolve. The athlete is also not dependent on the judges' subjective opinion, rather the ring numbers can actually be measured. It is a sport for every season and for every age.

Your child has started this sport, has already learned the very basics and wants to stick with it, train seriously with a club and be a part of a team. Do you know why? Ask your son or daughter about it or let him or her show you the page in this book that talks about motives. You can assume one thing: someone who trains in shooting sports wants to be successful and score high ring numbers.

This training book focuses on young shooting athletes during their initial years of training. It offers a lot of information about their sport, about technique, tactics and how to train properly. The young people will learn to better realize their own potential and to more consciously work with their body. This does not only promote more effective training but also prevents possible under- or over-training. The basic training and intermediate training are the same for all shooters, regardless of whether they will later remain recreational athletes or switch to performance-oriented clubs. For all of them this book provides orientation and support for successful training.

Training Shooting Sports

All parents, siblings, grandparents and friends can gain important information from this book. Use this book together with your children as a training companion, workbook and reference work. Surely you will occasionally be asked to help set goals, keep personal records or a training diary. Together with your young shooting athlete, enjoy his personal achievements and successful competitions. Adolescents need our approval, praise and recognition. Be sympathetic on those occasions when things aren't going well. Not everyone has what it takes to be a world-class shooter.

More than anything shooting sports are fun, promote social interaction, and develop ambition and perseverance. As they train and compete together adolescents learn to overcome their weaker inner-self and learn to deal with success and failure. Character traits such as self-discipline, sense of responsibility, reliability, punctuality, organization, perseverance, the willingness to take risks, courage and the desire to succeed, are cultivated and will also be useful in other areas of life.

Unfortunately shooting sports are sometimes misunderstood and equated with violence or militarism. We must categorically distance ourselves from that! The firearm is a piece of sports equipment like the javelin in track and field or the foil in fencing. The shot's only objective is to hit the center of the target and to score the highest ring numbers.